T0248185

PIRATE COVE

COVE

AN INSIDER'S ACCOUNT OF THE
INFAMOUS SOUTHPORT LANE SCANDAL

PIRATE COVE

AN INSIDER'S ACCOUNT OF THE INFAMOUS SOUTHPORT LANE SCANDAL

RICHARD D. BAILEY

PIRATE COVE

Cover design by Christine Van Bree
Interior design by Anita Dugan-Moore of Cyber Bytz, www.cyber-bytz.com

978-1-61088-612-3 HC
978-1-61088-613-0 PB
978-1-61088-614-7 Ebook
978-1-61088-615-4 Audio

Published by Bancroft Press
"Books that Enlighten"
(818) 275-3061
4527 Glenwood Ave.
La Crescenta, CA 91214
www.bancroftpress.com

Printed in the U.S.A.

CONTENTS

A true story

CHAPTER 1

October 29, 2021

I was driving home from Home Depot when my phone rang. It was the FBI special agent who'd led the federal investigation and prosecution of Alexander Chatfield Burns and others for the $350 million fraud they pulled off at Southport Lane, the company Burns had started and run.

The unplanned direct call from the agent struck me as odd. He'd always texted me before phoning. In fact, for years, our communicating had always followed this sequence: I'd get a text from him asking, "Have time for a quick call?" My text response was always "Sure" or "Yep." Within minutes, my phone would ring.

No text today. Just my phone screen lighting up with my entry for him: "Peter FBI."

The consummate southern gentleman, Peter first asked me how I was doing. His calls spiked my anxiety, and he knew it. As always, I said "fine" and nothing more. I just wanted to get down to business.

He said he wanted to give me a heads up before the news hit the media: "Alex Burns killed himself yesterday."

My first reaction was characteristically foul-mouthed. "Holy fuck!" I said.

My second, more considered, less profane reaction was: "I'm not surprised. Alex wasn't tough enough for prison."

***

A day or so later, *The Wall Street Journal* ran a big article on Alex's suicide at the age of thirty-four, and the raft of legal problems that followed him to his grave.

All I could think of was… what a waste. In a strange way, I kind of liked Alex. He'd been quick-witted and funny—even generous at times.

On second thought, maybe not generous at all. After all, it wasn't his money he was shoveling around.

***

When I first met Alex Burns, he was young (26), naïve, and not just insecure but constantly searching for affirmation from others.

He was also smart. No doubt about that. But not nearly as smart as he told everyone he was. He didn't want people to be impressed with him. He wanted them to be in awe of him. On more than one occasion, he said to me and others, "I'm always the smartest guy in the room." Just saying that about yourself seemed dumb to me.

Alex Burns was a complicated character. Wildly over his head, he had been surrounded by sycophants, grifters, and others trying to exploit his inexperience, gullibility, and checkbook.

And he was also a stone-cold liar.

I have a son whose name also is Alexander. At the time, Alexander Bailey had just started his freshman year at Yale. When Burns and I first met, the very first words out of his mouth was that he had gone to Yale too.

One night somewhat later, as we were sitting in Smith & Wollensky, a midtown Manhattan steak house popular with the Wall Street set, Alex Burns asked me to get my son Alex Bailey on the phone. So I did.

Burns proceeded to tell my son and me that he was such a rebel that he'd founded an alternative to Yale's storied secret societies. Instead of Skull & Bones, his was called "Porn & Chicken." He even asked my son to Google it. Sure enough, my son quickly found an old article on the website *Yale Daily News* about the university's new secret society and how it was making a pornographic movie starring none other than… Alex Burns.

There was only one problem. It was a different Alex Burns. The article in question had been published in 2002, when the Alex Burns sitting across the table from me, swilling the second of two very expensive bottles of wine, was all of about fifteen years old. I found out about his bold-faced lie soon after returning to my hotel room that night. My son, Alex, who had done a bit more Internet research, texted me to call bullshit on Burns' story.

Another time, Burns and I had a conversation about sailing—a longtime passion of mine—in which he told me he raced against a fleet of 60-foot boats off Westport, CT, where he grew up. But a few minutes into the conversation, it became clear he didn't know the flat end of a boat from the pointy end.

My son being Alex Bailey, and Burns being Alex Burns, they landed next to one another on my cell phone contact list. I joked about that once, and Alex Burns chimed in that he loved receiving texts from me signed, "Love, Dad." He really liked that story. He told it a lot.

But it never happened.

By the time of that shared steak dinner in the city, I'd already begun to catalogue my various concerns about Burns. A lot of strange things had been said by him and done by both him and others at Southport Lane. It was becoming clear this was not a "normal" private equity firm he was heading.

In November 2018, Alex Burns pled guilty to eight federal fraud charges. From 2018 to 2021, he apparently cooperated with Federal prosecutors as they subsequently indicted and got guilty pleas from other Southport players: Brian Gimelson, Robert McGraw, and ultimately the inheritor of the crumbling Southport empire, Burns' old partner, Andrew Scherr.

Brian Gimelson pled guilty to tax evasion charges. Seems he forgot to include a $1.2 million commission from Southport as income on his taxes. He was given early prison release during the COVID pandemic.

Rob McGraw pled guilty to misrepresenting $50 million in bogus securities as real and was sentenced to 18 months.

Andrew Scherr pled guilty to two counts of fraud and was sentenced to five years.

Alex Burns was scheduled to be sentenced on December 13, 2021, in the Southern District of New York. His usefulness to prosecutors was apparently over.

But forty-nine days before being sentenced, he killed himself in the Charleston, South Carolina home of his girlfriend.

A really smart friend of mine once asked Burns how he'd managed to gain control of three different insurance companies, and hence their millions of dollars in cash to invest. With a Cheshire cat grin, he cryptically answered, "Jesus with a telescope on Mars couldn't figure out how I did it."

Maybe not.

But I did.

CHAPTER 2

January 2013

I feel like my career is a big fat flop. I didn't plan on being a flop. No one does. But it kind of sneaks up on you.

You start your career full of piss and vinegar. Then twenty or thirty years go by, you look back, and you realize you ain't accomplished shit.

When I'm alone, which is far too often, I think back and go over many of the decisions I've made in my life up to this point. This accomplishes nothing. It doesn't change the outcomes or the lessons I've already learned. But I do it anyway. I wish I didn't.

I'm 55 years old, well-educated, and well-intentioned. I was raised in a wonderful, loving family. I have a wonderful wife and two great sons. We have a nice home in a beautiful leafy, seaside suburb of Boston. From that perspective, I'm a success. So no one should feel sorry for me.

But I have no job.

I think it's because my career premise stinks. I thought if I tackled, then solved big, complex, expensive business problems, the money would follow. You know… problems no one else would touch. Companies with bad problems. Companies no one would risk time and money on. The whole turning a sow's ear into a silk purse sort of thing. So, that is what I did. I tackled problems no one else would. To be fair to myself, I solved quite a few of them.

But it's been a while since I had a win.

On the successful ones, the money simply never showed up. Sure, I'd get good—sometimes great—mid-six-figure paychecks for a few years. But that was it. Once their companies were fixed, the owners would almost always come up with a reason to screw me.

Their prior promises of ownership, security, and profit-sharing were always just that—promises. Clearly, something my employers, investors, and clients had no issue ignoring. I hired more than my share of attorneys to settle these disputes. But the legal process just grinds both sides down until neither wants to fight anymore. Most of the time, I settled when I could no longer stomach the attorney's fees. Always for less than I was owed.

One time, I made my employer $3,000,000 in profit on an investment in a small company that got bought out by a large company 14 months after we made the investment. Three million dollars was our commission! The actual investor had put in $1,500,000, and a little over a year later took out $12,000,000. That adds up to an 800 percent return on investment. Pretty spectacular for only 14 months of risk.

I did *everything* on that deal. I found the investment, did all the due diligence on it. I sat on the board of directors. I attended dozens of meetings and was on hundreds of conference calls during the process of selling the company. I lived, breathed, and slept that little company the entire time.

Without our investors' money, the company would have been unable to deliver on its promises to its customer, one of the largest companies in the world. It would have cratered right then and there. Gone out of business. But we saved it. And made a ton of money in the process. How much did I get?

$100,000.

What happened to the other $2,900,000? Well, the partners of the firm divvied it up among themselves, probably over an expensive meal of red wine, steak, and strippers at the Diamond Cabaret, their favorite strip joint/steakhouse in Denver. Then they bought and refurbished their office building. It was a beautiful building. I was in it once. They don't own it anymore. Someone told me it was sold in foreclosure.

Don't get me wrong; I was grateful for the $100k. My wife and I had just bought a house. We had two little kids and my wife had not yet gone back to work.

So, when that $100,000 was deposited into my checking account, I took myself out for a proper wet lunch, walked in the door that night with a big smile, and loudly proclaimed, "Daddy's home!"

CHAPTER 3

A few years later, I started my own investment company. I was tired of being taken advantage of. It had become crystal clear that guys at the end of their careers do not care who they screw over. I'd relied enough on Wall Street's aging crocodiles. So, from here on in, I'd be making money for myself and my investors. I was ready to take charge.

We got off to a great start. I found a great partner, recruited solid board members, a top-notch law firm, auditors... everything. Then I found a small hedge fund in New York City to back us.

We had good, experienced people with verifiable track records (a must to raise money), lots of experience, and a committed capital source.

We were all set and on our way.

The first investment we made was in the semiconductor industry. The company was run by the same guy I'd invested in at my previous job. He pocketed $7 or $8 million in the previous deal. He was now well known in the industry. He was a hale fellow, hearty well met. Everyone liked him. I liked him. Still do.

But things in the new investment got off to a slow start. He was making headway, but not nearly at the rate he'd predicted prior to investing in him again. Then this little thing called the Great Recession kicked in.

You know that old saying: When So-and-So gets a cold, you get pneumonia? Well, that was us. It turns out our hedge fund backer—and now 70 percent owner of our investment firm—had a whole lot of funky investments in his portfolio.

In the space of a few months, his assets under management lost something like 80 percent of their value. It turns out he got pneumonia.

We died.

CHAPTER 4

I was sidelined for over a year cleaning up that firm's mess. There was no money to pay anyone, least of all me. In fact, I was draining my savings to keep my dream-turned-nightmare alive.

In our business, your reputation is only as good as your last deal, and if your last deal ended up in the shitter, guess what? Your value in the industry goes right down the bowl with it.

People who thought I was great two years ago now thought I sucked. No one called me. No one e-mailed me.

It was like I'd died.

Until someone has a really bad deal that needs cleaning up, no one will touch you. Then someone remembers you're at home, sitting on your ass.

Finally, your phone rings.

CHAPTER 5

Late March 2013

I look down at my iPhone. It's a call from my old buddy Jeff. A good guy. Probably just checking up on me to make sure I haven't gone over the edge. Jeff is good like that.

I've done a lot of business with Jeff. He's a fascinating guy. He knows people with boatloads of money. Over the years, he's introduced me to some of my favorite people—the ones I respect and admire the most—as well as some of my close friends.

Jeff is about 6'4" and 300 pounds, an absolute mountain of a man. Well-dressed in expensive suits and Hermes ties, he can press the flesh with the best of them. He's smart, makes everyone laugh, and almost always insists on picking up the tab at some of the finest restaurants in the country—his preferred meeting places.

Jeff makes introductions. If something works out, he gets a piece of the action. If not, there's always another introduction to make. But he does know some "interesting" people. Some real beauties. You know, the kind of people who walk into a room looking like a million after taxes but are actually one wrong move away from bankruptcy.

Now, everyone in finance and investments has met these types of guys. They talk a huge game, often falling back on phrases like "I guarantee it" and "You can't lose." But they don't guarantee it, and you will lose. Trust me.

Eventually, you develop your own detection system or gut instinct when you meet these guys. I call mine the "sleaze meter." If my sleaze meter went off in a meeting, I was done. I'd either become super cautious or, even more often, I'd mentally shut down.

11

One time, when I was living in Los Angeles. Jeff and I were driving home after taking a potential investor to dinner at Spago in Beverly Hills. Early in the evening, my sleaze meter went off the charts on this guy.

I said to Jeff, "Dude, there has to be a crime involved here."

"What do you mean?" Jeff asked.

"There has to be a crime here. This guy is too stupid to have all that money," I answered.

Sure enough, a few years later, he went to prison for ten or so years. Seems he was getting AIDS patients to take out life insurance policies and listing his company as the beneficiary when they died. Only problem was, he was hiding from the insurance companies the fact that the patient was terminally ill. No one ever said insurance people were smart.

Sometime during the '90s, Jeff and I ran up a $1,500 tab at a sushi joint in L.A. It wasn't even an expensive sushi joint. We were with a client, a tech guy. We did not have the faintest idea what his company did. So, we put on a show instead. Jeff is fun.

A few weeks later, I told the guy over dinner in Connecticut—it was just the two of us—that, in good conscience, I could not put him into the deal. It was not in his best interests.

It would have been great for us. But the company I was running at the time was a horror show. His company, well-managed and pristine, was making money.

Merging with our company would just force him into solving and paying for all our problems. He loved me for that ever since.

I never told Jeff.

CHAPTER 6

Phone conversations with Jeff frequently start with the two of us saying some nasty shit to each other. It lightens the mood.

This time was no different.

I grabbed my phone, hit the accept button, and immediately said, "Yo. You callin' to see if I've got the gun in my mouth yet?"

Jeff's response was just as brutal: "No, and shut the fuck up, you miserable half-Irish bastard. I'm calling you with some good news if you can get your fat head out of your stupid ass."

"Ooh!" I replied, a small smile beginning to cross my face. "I think I'm getting aroused! What's up?"

Now, it seems Jeff had just started working at a private equity firm that no one had ever heard of called Southport Lane. Now when I say no one had ever heard of them, I mean like… they sprang from nowhere.

Most private equity firms have a well-respected Wall Street type at the top. Someone with a track record that investors—like pension funds, banks, insurance companies, etc.—can trust. Someone whose deals over the years you can thoroughly investigate spend months and sometimes years investigating their background and pulling apart every deal they have done to make sure they worked. Investors want to know that if they gave this guy's firm $10 million, $15 million, or even $50 million dollars, that:

a. They would get their money back and
b. They would earn a big fat return on their investment.

When you look at new private equity firms, you expect to see an ex-Goldman Sachs guy or someone from Bain Capital or KKR (Kohlberg Kravis Roberts & Co), with years of big deal experience and huge financial relationships striking out on their own after years making deals for others.

Southport Lane had none of that.

"Check this out," Jeff says. "The 26-year-old kid who runs this place just asked me to be president of the entire firm. The place has a billion under management," he continues. "He owns two or three insurance companies, and we get to invest the excess cash on the insurance companies' balance sheets," he finishes with obvious excitement.

Incredulous and baffled, I stammered out an underwhelming, "Uh, congratulations… I guess?"

Now, to know Jeff is to love Jeff as well as to be constantly amazed and amused at how he glides effortlessly from one big paying job to another. He once confessed to me that the secret to his success is that he "only needs to deliver on 51 percent of his bullshit."

But seriously, I've known him for over 20 years. I've worked closely with him for many of those, and there are two things Jeff is not—a CEO or a private equity guy. Take my word for it. Jeff's a sales guy, a relationship guy, and he's very good at that stuff.

But Jeff doesn't do details, nor does he manage people. That's where I come in.

"Wait," I say, my professional skepticism beginning to kick in. "Twenty-six years old? Who the hell is this kid, and how does he wind up managing a billion dollars?"

"It's an amazing story," Jeff continues. "He's like some prodigy who's been running money for years."

"This makes no sense," my voice stiffening. "Where'd he get the money?"

"No idea where he got the original cash—probably family money. He's from an old WASP family in Connecticut. Goes all the way back to the Mayflower. But he now owns a bunch of insurance companies, and he wants me to run their private equity investments," Jeff says.

"What's his name?" I ask.

"Get this!" Jeff giggled before affecting his best Locust Valley lockjaw. "His name is Alexander Chatfield Burns."

"Never heard of him," I said.

None of it made any sense to me. But what do I know? I'm unemployed. I've been out of work for more than a year, which feels like an eternity. I feel like I'm rapidly becoming a non-entity, a ghost. Maybe the world, in the interim, has fundamentally changed.

But after a year of being home and staring out the window, I feel like I've fallen so far behind. I'm angry at myself and the world. My last deal was a bust. I'm damaged goods. I'm going to wind up pumping gas and telling myself, "All work has dignity."

What a bunch of bullshit!

Jeff interrupts this familiar, "the world's not fair" recitation going on inside my head.

"Now listen," he says, starting to show some irritability. "Stop pissing on everything. I've been talking to the guys at a pharmaceutical company in New Jersey. We—and by 'we' I mean Southport—have pretty much made a deal to buy a controlling interest in them. Now we need someone to go to their facility and do due diligence for us. I don't trust any of the morons here to do that, and as you know, I'm not good at that shit."

"I'm listening," I say. "Go on."

"We'll pay you $5,000 a week plus expenses. If we do the deal, we'll put you in as Chief Operating Officer or Chief Financial Officer, and maybe you won't be such a miserable prick every time I dial your number."

"I'm in. I'm in," I interrupt. "When do I go?"

"Next week," he answers. "After you're done, you'll come into the city, meet with the guys here, and we'll go get a proper dinner."

I hang up the phone and look over at my long-suffering wife of 20 years, on the couch across the room. She's a teacher and is correcting papers. Having overheard the entire conversation, she looks over her glasses and simply says, "Buh-bye," with a slightly exaggerated wave.

I've been home a long time.

CHAPTER 7

Jersey Pharmaceutical Corp.
Northern New Jersey

Walking into Jersey Pharmaceutical Corp is like walking into a 1950s time capsule.

The first thing you notice is the sheer size of the place. It's huge. It has the look of a warehouse from the industrial revolution that was painted over and remodeled into an Eisenhower-era mega-department store.

Today, the parking lot, which is located next to a highway overpass with trucks rumbling noisily overhead, is half empty.

To get inside, you pass through an old swivel door and are immediately gob-smacked by a cavernous three-story lobby with a tiny reception desk sitting off to your right and a small waiting area with a couple of seats and a couch about thirty yards away to your left. Ice it over, and you could play an NHL game in the lobby.

Seriously, you really wonder if the receptionist is going to have to grab a bullhorn to call your name when it's time for your appointment. The place is that big.

The most eye-popping thing of all is about 200 feet in front of you—an enormous escalator between the first and second floors, just like the ones you saw in a Macy's or JC Penny in the 1960s and 1970s. You know, before revenue per square foot was a measure of efficiency.

The next thing you notice is that there's only one escalator. Aren't there usually two? One for up and one for down? Not here. Just one.

Strange place.

CHAPTER 8

It's 9:35 am when an intercom calls out my name. I'm the only one in the convention center-sized lobby, so I chuckle to myself. A few seconds go by, and the CEO, an elderly gent nattily dressed—pocket kerchief and everything—comes out a side door I didn't even notice.

He introduces himself. His name is Jerry, and he invites me to tour the facility with him. I immediately ask him. "Why is there only one escalator?"

"It goes both ways," he tells me. "In the morning, we turn it to go up. In the afternoon, we turn it to go down. That way we don't have people crowding the staircase. Fire safety, you know."

I'm thoroughly baffled, but I mutter, "Makes sense."

Actually, it didn't. Who operates an escalator to make the fire chief happy?

We go for a walk around the building. He takes me through the accounting department, the manufacturing floor, shipping and receiving, purchasing, and again the accounting department. I'm not sure he understands that we already went through the accounting department.

Once again, I'm struck by the enormity of the building and its cavernous nature. There's one employee every fifty feet or so.

Finally, we meet the people who really run the place—Jerry's two daughters and their best friend, the CFO.

Now, Jeff never told me this, but apparently, the two daughters and the CFO are not Jeff's biggest fans. So, when Jerry says, "Jeff introduced us, and Richard is here to look things over in preparation for that big investment from Jeff's firm I told you about," they withdraw their hands from the obligatory shake. Except for the CFO. She slips me the dead-fish shake. No smile.

During that uncomfortable moment, I realize that the whistling sound Jerry makes when speaking is because his dentures don't fit right.

Now, *normally*, when you're representing a potential investor in someone's company, the sellers treat you nicely. Not here. Not at Jersey Pharma. Jerry was nice. But the daughters and the CFO were hostile and cold. They had known I was coming for almost a week.

As agreed, I had arrived at 9:00 am that Monday, having come down from Boston the night before, and expecting to plunge into work right away. You know, the usual due diligence stuff. Financial statement review, inventory review, talks with folks who work on the shop floor, etc.

Not exactly exciting work. It's more of a grind. The whole object is to learn what makes this place tick and why. Or, as is frequently the case, why is this place in trouble, and should it be saved? Not could it be saved, but *should* it be saved?

After more stilted and uncomfortable chit-chat, I ask the group about their availability to spend a few hours with me. Suddenly, they're all busy and unable to commit to a date and time. Except for Jerry, who breaks the tension by offering to show me the conference room I'll be working in for the week.

When you show up at a company which is clearly struggling— one that needs new capital to survive—and the top managers say they're too busy to meet with you, right there you know that management is most likely the problem. Right there, you know things ain't right, that they've got something to hide.

When I told Jerry that his girls and the CFO were "too busy" to meet, he interceded. It seemed one daughter owned a bar in Manhattan. The other one had an office in a nearby building where she ran a separate business selling some of Dad's products under a different company name. The CFO? She wanted nothing to do with me.

But thanks to Jerry, we set up meetings for Wednesday and Thursday morning with "the girls," as he refers to them.

As the noon hour approached, Jerry asked me if I was hungry. I said "yes" because I was. A cordial host, Jerry asked if I liked Italian food.

Now, I'm from New Haven. While my family background is English, Irish, and German, many of my friends growing up were Italian. Nothing puts a smile on my face like the thought of going to a good Italian restaurant. Especially if it reminded me of my friends' kitchens. Especially when their mothers and grandmothers were cooking Sunday dinner. They loved feeding me. Actually… they loved feeding everyone.

"Great," Jerry replied. "I know a good place nearby. Have you ever heard of Benito's?"

"No" I replied. "But I'm from New Haven, so I have high standards," I added, trying to be cordial and light.

"You'll love this place," Jerry added. "I'm surprised you haven't heard of it. I have a meeting after lunch. Let's take two cars. Just follow me."

So I did. A few minutes later, we're at Benito's. When Jerry walked in, no one said a word. We weren't greeted. We weren't led to a table. Jerry just walked in, went to a table by the window, which had a lovely view of a quiet street, and sat down.

Benito's is a classic New York-style Italian restaurant, even down to the mural of some fictional Italian Valhalla on one of the walls. I've been in a thousand of these types of joints. They hand you huge menus covered in plastic, and they have about three wait-staff for every patron.

But one thing was certain. The food would be so stupendous it would remind me of meals eaten at my friend Mike's house. We were best friends growing up. Still are.

On any given Sunday growing up, Mike's mother and grandmother could bank on seeing me come through the door. Then they'd break into huge smiles and say, "Richie, come sit down. Let me make you a plate." I loved it.

Mike and I played football together from fifth grade through high school. Shortly after we met, he invited me over one Sunday for dinner. I'll never forget it. Six years later, the minute I got my driver's license, I started to regularly show up at the Palaises' house on Sundays. Then I'd go home for dinner at my house, where a huge pile of beef, fat dripping down its sides from being in the oven for four hours, was our standard Sunday meal.

Sorry, Mom, but roast beef and pan-browned potatoes never quite equaled meatballs and sauce by Mike Palaia's mother and grandmother. Just sayin'.

Jerry didn't say a word to the restaurant staff. They brought over a glass of wine for him.

They looked at me. "Water is fine," I said. I was trying to make a good impression.

It was now clear to me that Jerry was very much a regular at Benito's. He ordered for me but not for himself. They brought him a small plate of something and about five pounds of food for me. Not gonna lie. The food was fantastic.

Jerry and I really didn't talk business until the end of lunch. We chatted about ordinary things. Friends, families, current events. But when we did turn to business, I went with the flow and let Jerry talk while I listened and hope the wine would provide me with some useful illumination.

I did learn a few things. First, Jerry doesn't do details—the girls do that—and second, the entire company was bankrolled by a buddy of his—Carl. I knew who Carl was—basically a billionaire who owned and sold a huge chain of companies. He and Jerry have been friends for decades. By supporting Jersey Pharmaceutical, Carl was doing his old pal a solid.

When lunch was over and the friendly chit-chat done, Jerry, who was now two or three glasses of wine deep, partially soaked up by maybe 300 calories of food, announced he had to head to his afternoon meeting. No check arrived. Just a bag for me filled with the leftovers from what I couldn't eat for lunch. "I'll see you tomorrow," Jerry said.

I went back to my hotel. The only thing I'd really learned from my first day was that Jerry was a regular at Benito's, that "the girls" were really in charge of the day-to-day, and that they wanted no part of dealing with me.

CHAPTER 9

Regarding Southport's contemplated investment in Jersey Pharmaceutical, there's definitely some sort of disconnect. Jeff is saying it's a great deal. Jerry is saying that they really need the money. The girls are treating me like a leper.

The CFO was openly hostile. The Manhattan nightclub owner gave me exactly twelve minutes. The other daughter told me that everything was fine and told me to speak with her sister or the CFO.

Every day was the same. I'd get there at 9:00 am. Sit down at the workspace they gave me. Request information from the CFO—most of which was never provided—and around 11:30 am, Jerry would ask me if I was hungry. So, off to Benito's we would go.

By Wednesday, I was matching him glass for glass. He would then leave me for his afternoon meeting, and I'd take a bag full of killer Italian food back to my hotel for dinner, where I'd write my observations in preparation for the deal memorandum I'd eventually have to present to the folks at Southport.

Nothing was exciting about this deal. It made no sense. In fact, it stunk.

Here's what I saw.

1. Yes. They were losing money, but not enough to go out of business.

2. Jerry, the CEO, was a charming man. He was a consummate gentleman who left all the business details to his daughters and the CFO. His real job? Keeping Carl, the billionaire mogul, happy, so when they needed more money, Carl would write them a big check.

3. There was nothing truly special about this company. If it went out of business, probably no one would care.

I was due at Southport Lane's offices on Madison Avenue on Friday. I pushed it up to Thursday afternoon because there was nothing of value to be gained from another day at Jersey Pharmaceutical.

CHAPTER 10

Thursday finally rolls around, and there I am at 9:00 am, sitting on the couch with plastic-covering in the cavernous waiting room, staring at that ridiculous escalator which I've yet to see move. Turns out it was broken, and they couldn't afford to repair it. Kind of summed up my experience at Jersey Pharma.

Jerry finally comes out of the side door. Sharply dressed as ever, he greets me like we're old friends. I guess we are after a few liquid lunches. But I'd not put a dime in his company based on anything he says. Besides, he's got his buddy Carl. He doesn't need Southport.

We go into his office and shoot the shit some more. No real talk of business. He's a proud father, and he's going on about how wonderful, smart, and talented his daughters are and how they're "good kids." I'm happy for him. Really.

But I didn't bring up how badly I'm bruised from the ten-foot pole "the girls" have been using to keep me away, and how basically rude they were to me. Best to keep my mouth shut until I get out of here, which I hope is soon.

When the subject does finally switch to business, he emphasizes how this company would have gone out of business if it weren't for his daughters. "They know everything about this place. They grew up here," Jerry goes on. "This place would sink without them."

I thought to myself: One daughter is playing Manhattan nightclub impresario, and the other is running her own business out of a hard-to-find shed. Getting information from the CFO is damn near impossible.

This place has lost $54 million over the years. It would already have been resting at the bottom of the sea if it weren't for Carl bailing out their sinking ship. Someone must have photos of him somewhere doing things he shouldn't have been doing.

But I keep my mouth shut. My job is to report back to Southport, and in a few hours, that's exactly what I was going to do.

At about 11:30 am, Jerry says, "Oops! Where'd the time go? I have an appointment for lunch, so I'll walk you out."

As we head out into the parking lot, Jerry starts getting chummy and throws his arm around my shoulders.

"So, how long before you think we can close this investment?" he asks.

"Oh, I don't know," I respond. "That's up to Southport. I'm heading there for a meeting now so I'm sure someone will be in touch with you shortly. I'm just a contractor for the week."

Clearly, he has no idea that Southport wants to buy a majority share of the company and replace the CFO and either one or both of his daughters… with me apparently.

Southport isn't looking to make an investment. I'm pretty sure they're looking to make "a pig move," which isn't a formal term in business, but one everybody understands. It means get everything for as little as possible, put in your own management, skinny the place down, and suck all the cash out in the form of dividends and fees.

There's only one problem: Jerry can always go to his buddy Carl. He doesn't need Southport, and in my professional opinion, Southport doesn't need Jersey Pharmaceutical.

CHAPTER 11

Within five minutes of pulling out of the parking lot, the lower Manhattan skyline smacks you in the face. I've always felt that there's more opportunity on one block of Manhattan than there is in the rest of America. Every time I get to see that view, it makes me smile. It's like having all your hopes and dreams suddenly flash before your eyes.

Until you hit the traffic.

The easiest way for me to come into the city is through the Holland Tunnel. When it was completed in 1927, the tunnel was 1.62 miles long, 20 feet wide, and 93 feet below the surface of the Hudson River.

So let's do a little math: In 1927, there were around 27 million cars in the United States, and the U.S. had a population of approximately 119 million people. That equates to about one car for every five people. But in 2013, there are about 255 million cars—almost 10 times the 1927 total—and about 316 million people in the good ol' USA.

That means that almost 80 percent of a population that has DOUBLED now owns a car, and it feels like all of them are trying to get from New Jersey to Manhattan at the very same moment I am.

But it's not traffic *in* the tunnel that's so infuriating. It's the traffic trying to get to the tunnel. I've seen signs for the tunnel for the last 45 minutes, but the entrance is nowhere in sight.

I hate being late. Somewhere in my formative years, it was drilled into me that being late was rude and disrespectful. While I'm pretty even-tempered, when I fear being late, anger and anxiety rise quickly in me. It's the shortest distance between me and losing my temper that I know. Then I can get a little hostile and aggressive. But when

I'm on time, I get a little thrill out of being perfectly on time—like down to the second. It's annoying to everybody. But I get a kick out of it.

I was supposed to be at Southport's offices at 2:00 pm. I was going to try and check into my hotel, and park the car, first. I was only carrying my briefcase (backpack, actually) because I figured we'd be hitting some bar or major steak house—or both—at the end of the day and I didn't want to be lugging my carry-bag, which was now full of dirty clothes.

But to be honest, I wanted to look like I belonged in mid-town Manhattan. Not like some tourist or conference attendee.

It was now almost 1:00 pm. I'd left Jersey Pharma almost an hour and a half earlier, and I'm not even at the tunnel yet. I'm close, but at this rate, I'm going to be not just a little late. I'm going to be really late, and I'm getting pissed off about it. I want to make a good impression. Who knows what could come of this? Maybe another assignment. Maybe even a full-time job. I need both right now.

Finally, I see the entrance to the tunnel. But who knows how long it will take to get through? And then I have to drive about 30 blocks north, find a garage, bolt to the hotel, check-in, check my bag, and then walk a few blocks to Southport's office at 45th and Madison Ave. I also didn't want to walk in there looking like a harried idiot. This was important. I could feel the anger heating up inside me.

There was no way I was going to make it. Thankfully, I've got Jeff on speed dial. I hit his number and he answers right away.

"Hey, what's up?' he says.

"How the fuck do you people live like this?" I blurt out. Clearly my traffic-induced anxiety had not subsided.

"What the fuck are talking about, Ass-wipe?" Jeff responds. "Where are you?"

"I'm gonna be late. I'm just entering the tunnel now. It took me an hour and a half to get this far," I explain as my volatility tamps down. "I'm going to be at least a half-hour late. No way around it."

"Don't worry about it. Get here when you get here. Besides, these Jamokes around here can't do anything on time anyway, so settle the fuck down, drop your car and your shit at the hotel, and come on over. In the meantime, let me see if I can get them to cut a check for you, ok?"

"A check? Haven't seen one of those for a while. It'll be nice to walk in the door with one again," I add.

"Yeah, well don't tell your wife just yet. Nothing around here ever happens the way it's supposed to, but I don't want you walking in the door at home with just a hangover to show for this week," Jeff says. "Don't break a sweat over this meeting. I'll see you when you get here." The phone goes dead.

Ooooh, a check, I say to myself as I immediately dial home with the good news. I get voicemail and tell my wife I'm heading into the city to meet these guys and to have dinner. I don't mention the check. It kills me. But I don't.

CHAPTER 12

By the grace of someone's god, I hit the entrance to the tunnel and the traffic eases up. We're moving steadily now. By steady, I mean we're going 20 miles per hour, but it feels like we're racing.

So basically, the previous hour and forty-five minutes were caused by twenty or thirty thousand cars consolidating from about nine lanes down to two in the space of about a quarter of a mile. This, in a nutshell, is the problem with New York, just as it is with other, old, eastern industrialized cities. The infrastructure sucks. Being in New York is fun. Getting in and out of it is a pain in the ass. Same for Boston, Philadelphia, and Chicago.

But 88 years ago, when they finished this tunnel, they never imagined the armada of Chevy Suburbans, Lincoln Navigators, or Cadillac Escalades bombing down this narrow tunnel. No, the first cars that went under the Hudson River from New Jersey to Manhattan in 1927 probably could have fit in the back seat of some of these monstrous SUVs.

There also seems to be this unwritten rule that as they try to pass me safely, I must actively confront the possibility of crashing into the tunnel wall.

I don't like these tunnels. I never have. When I was a kid, we went in and out of Manhattan and Long Island using the Midtown tunnel all the time. My grandparents lived in New York City and spent the summers on Long Island, and we visited a lot. But it spooked me to no end that there were boats and ships above us. Seeing puddles on the tunnel roads didn't help either.

My favorite part of the tunnel was, then and now, when you start to go up. That means you'll be out soon. Mercifully, I hit the daylight ahead and turned left to head uptown.

Southport Lane's offices were in Midtown East, at Madison Ave. and 44th Street. I'd worked at 400 Madison—one block north—about 10 years earlier, so I knew the area well. About a block up from Southport was JP Morgan's world headquarters, which they got for practically nothing when Bear Stearns went under in 2008, kicking off the Great Financial Crisis.

Across the street from Southport was the venerable Yale Club of New York. One block from there was the architectural magic of Grand Central Station. This is prime mid-town Manhattan office territory. You had to be managing a shitload of cash just to get a commercial real estate agent to return your call. Hell, the security deposit to lease a bathroom in this part of town had to be at least $500,000.

I rolled into a familiar parking garage across the street from Southport's office. Got out, flipped the keys to the attendant, put the ticket in my wallet, and crossed over onto the west side of Madison Avenue.

I walked past the Brooks Brothers flagship store and a bunch of other men's high-end clothing stores. J. Press, my favorite, being a New Haven guy, was less than half a block away on 44th Street. This was familiar ground to me.

My grandfather used to get his suits custom made at FR Tipler right around the corner. In 1984 or thereabouts, I splurged on a beige cashmere topcoat there. When getting fitted, I told the guy doing the measurements that my grandfather had been a customer. He asked me his name, squinted, and said: "Harry Arnold. Goldman Sachs. I remember him. He had a colostomy bag, so we made his suits larger on one side."

Yep. That was him. He died in 1968. I thought dropping his name might get me a legacy discount price. Not a chance. But hey, I tried.

I still have the coat.

Just ahead was the doorway to 350 Madison Ave.

I roll through the revolving door and head to the security desk to check in. As they scan my driver's license, I check out the building directory and see that Southport Lane has the entire 21st floor. I'm in the right place and I'm only 15 minutes late, which is on-time by Manhattan standards. So far so good.

Security hands me my building pass and directs me to an elevator bank that'll take me up the 21 flights.

Just before the door opens on 21, I indulge my habit—picked up from Roy Scheider's portrayal of choreographer Bob Fosse in "All That Jazz"—by looking into the mirror, extending out the palms of my hands, and quietly saying, "Showtime." It's silly. But it helps me put my game face on.

The doors open to a nice reception area. Above the receptionist's desk is a bold proclamation of where we are:

SOUTHPORT LANE
PRIVATE EQUITY • ASSET MANAGEMENT

I introduce myself to the receptionist. "Good afternoon. Richard Bailey to see Jeff, please."

A moment later, Jeff ambles around the corner, sees me, and says, "Commodore? Glad to see you made it. Come on in. I'll show you around."

There are other people nearby, so we're professional and polite to each other. Not our usual asshole selves. Which is a rarity. Jeff and I've talked shit to each other since shortly after we met. Neither of us means it. We're just trying to make each other laugh.

As we walk around the corner, the first thing I see is a big, long room with a typical Wall Street trading desk. It has seats for maybe 20 to 25 traders and salespeople. I then notice that the room is ringed by offices with floor-to-ceiling windows facing the trading area. There are probably eight to ten people sitting at the trading desk. But it's still a nice setup. All the offices are occupied.

On the walls are old stock certificates, expensively framed. Nice touch. My father, a former Merrill Lynch and then Smith Barney guy, had been collecting old stock certificates for about 40 years. He had a couple hundred of them, some of which went back more than a century. Recently, some New Hampshire collector bought his entire collection.

I smirked wondering if any of these belonged to my dad.

Could be. Who knows? Anyway, what pops into my mind is that either these Southport guys come from old-money, or they're doing a fantastic job of trying to look like they come from old-money.

"Wow!" I remark to Jeff. "This place is busy. You guys must be doing a shitload of business to pay for this setup."

"We do a shitload of something. But to tell the truth, I have no idea what half these folks do."

This strikes me as very odd. Jeff is the president of this entire firm, and he doesn't know what half these people do or how they contribute? I guess I'm not terribly surprised. Jeff isn't a details guy. But I couldn't sit in his office and stare out at all these people, day in and day out, without needing to find out just what the hell they were doing and why. It's just my nature.

As we walk around the perimeter of the trading floor, I notice that every single office door ringing the area is shut. In a couple of the offices, two to three guys seem to be deep in conversation. They're all standing, and every door is firmly shut.

After we do what seems like a full 360-degree walk around the office, Jeff and I amble into the conference room. It's beautiful. Fabulous midtown Manhattan views. A big conference table with seats for probably fifteen. The huge, *de-rigueur* flat-screen TV on the wall with CNBC on but sound muted. A nice credenza with various sodas and snacks neatly set up on top. Nice glassware, too. Off to the left is a little refrigerator with a glass door filled with wine bottles laying on their sides. On the walls are more antique stock certificates, neatly framed.

Everything about this room says they're managing a lot of fucking money.

I sit down at the middle of the table with my back to the outdoor window. My sons call it the Gotti seat. It's a habit. I like to see everyone coming into or going out of the room. That way no one sneaks up on me. Jeff sits on the other side, closer to the head of the table.

About four or five people make their way into the conference room. They range in age from mid-30s to mid-40s. All male, all white. All wearing variations of the same uniform: dark slacks, light blue formal shirt, no tie, open collar, no jacket. Some sport French cuffs with cufflinks. Some don't. I'm in your basic Brooks Brothers dark gray suit, white shirt, and muted but fashionable tie. I'm decidedly over-dressed for this group. That's ok. I'm trying to convey the fact that I'm older and wiser. It's a habit. I don't think it matters. No one cares anymore.

We shake hands, exchange cards, and make perfunctory niceties while we wait for the big cheese to show up.

Suddenly, all goes silent as a thin, balding man walks in. No smile. I didn't really see him come in but, as he enters, suddenly everyone sort of stops their conversations and starts to look down at their phones. He walks over to me, extends his hand, and introduces himself.

"I'm Andrew, Alex's partner," he says smoothly and confidently. He hands me his card. His name is Andrew Scherr, and his card says he's the Chief Financial Officer.

I'm thinking… okay. So, this guy is probably the hammer in the organization. The enforcer. That's why everyone went silent when he walked in the door.

Whoever he is, the mood in the room went from easy-going to tense the moment he stepped in.

Now, you know how you get an instant warning sign about someone when you first meet them? That's what I got from Andrew. I immediately tensed up. This guy came off as controlled, calibrated, and tightly wound. He was extremely polite, courtly even, almost in that perfunctory southern way. But even his courtliness felt staged, controlled.

While everyone else was dressed in varying forms of business casual, he was the only Southport guy in a suit and tie.

When meeting someone who throws off that persona, my default reaction is to fall back on what I hope is an implacable suit of armor: good manners. Which is precisely what I do. Mine, I hope, do not carry the same undercurrent of menace that Andrew's do.

Chit-chat time in Southport Lane's conference room is officially over. Everyone takes a seat. All the Southport people are on one side. I'm alone on the other. No problem. I'm used to that.

No one has said a word since Scherr came into the room. Not a word, not even Jeff. Everyone is now staring down at their iPhones, which they hold in their laps. I think that's rude. To me, they're saying they have things more important to do than attend this meeting. But no one cares. This is the age of the iPhone. Staring down at your phone screen is a wonderful way to pretend you're busy, or even better, more important than everyone else.

I guess we're all waiting for Alex Burns, the chief strategist and majority shareholder of Southport Lane. The 26-year-old wunderkind.

I have to say, I'm curious as hell.

Then while staring at the array of cards in front of me, I notice something. Everyone has big titles—Jeff is President, another guy is CEO, Scherr is CFO, one other guy is an Executive Director, another fellow is head of something else. But they all sit in total silence waiting for a 26-year-old who, at a normal firm, would be a trainee or junior associate.

Weird.

CHAPTER 13

Suddenly, everyone on the other side of the table looks up from their phones, as if on command, and within a second or two, a twenty-something mess bursts into the room.

My first impression of Alexander Chatfield Burns: He's... awkward. He looks like he's power-walking faster than his legs can carry him, and that he'll pitch over, face first, at any moment. It doesn't help that he's staring down at his phone as he walks. In fact, I'm surprised he didn't walk straight into the side of the door, then fall into the room.

His reddish-brown hair could have used at least a comb if not a wash. He wore an expensive shirt, rumpled and partially untucked, with French cuffs and unremarkable cufflinks. He could have used a shave too.

Without even looking up or saying a word to anyone, Burns goes to the snacks arranged neatly on the credenza, rifles through them, scrambles them, finds nothing he wants, turns around, and says to no one in particular, "Why don't we have anything healthy here?"

No one answers. Burns turns around from the now messy snack layout. He looks sideways toward me.

With no introduction, he immediately starts talking while staring at his phone.

"Jeff tells me your son is a Classics major at Yale. I was a Classics major at Yale too. Until I got thrown out for running a hedge fund from my dorm room. Fucking Dave Swenson, the head of Yale's Endowment, didn't like it that my returns were beating his."

Now arriving is my second impression of him. To say Alex Burns is "extremely unorthodox" is a nice way of putting it. But most importantly, he wants you to know he's insanely smart.

He never introduces himself to me, and I do not introduce myself to him. I guess there's no need for such common business formalities at this point.

"Really?" I reply.

What else do you say to that? I was born and raised in New Haven. Worked in the Mayor's office during the early 1980s. I knew a ton of folks who went to Yale, including, of course, my own son. But I'd never heard anyone wave their Yale degree as if it were some sort of baseball bat to the head of mere mortals.

Then I think to myself, *Good Lord, I hope my son never acts like that.*

Burns sits down at the head of the conference table.

"So, should I buy Jersey Pharma?"

"No," I blurt out. I didn't mean to be so blunt, but I suddenly feel like I'm talking to one of my sons.

"Why not?" Burns fires back.

"Because you're going to lose all your money," I say.

I'm suddenly rethinking my bluntness. I'd not even talked this over with Jeff and have just blindsided him. Never a smart move. Jeff's a good guy and doesn't deserve this. Especially from me. Even more unwise in the current circumstance is the fact that I really need to get paid.

Burns is now glaring at Jeff. It's either an "I told you so" glare or a "You're an idiot" glare. Either way, I feel badly for Jeff. He's done me a favor, and I just ratfucked him.

I'm now knee-deep in crap of my own creation, and the tension level in the room has gone through the roof. Now nobody is looking at their phones. They're all staring directly at me. It really is showtime.

I look over at Jeff, and he's giving me a "what the fuck?" look. Then the thought flashes through my mind: *I've pissed off everyone, and now I'll be driving back to Boston without a check. How am I going to ex-plain that to my wife?* I can feel my face blush from my own stupidity and embarrassment. I should not have said what I'd just said.

With a mischievous grin, Burns looks over at Jeff but says to me, "Whaddya mean? Jeff told me this is a great deal. What are we missing here?"

I figure I'm fucked now, so my answer is going to be direct. Forget the business analysis; forget the financial analysis. The company had loads of problems that could be fixed. But that wasn't the real problem. Management was the real problem, and apparently someone at Southport had promised that the family members would keep their jobs. To get things right, however, the CFO, in my opinion, would have to be replaced.

So, I lean forward and level my gaze at Mr. Whiz Kid. "First," I say quietly but sternly, "this is a family business, meaning that every Sunday, every holiday, every wedding, every bar mitzvah—literally every occasion they get together as a family—they're going to have an informal board meeting and you'll not be there."

"Second," I say, "they don't care that they're losing money as long as they can find another investor to pony up some dough, which occasionally goes to a good business use, but mostly just goes to finance their nice, comfortable lifestyles."

"Third," I add, "they don't lose enough money to go out of business. They only lose enough to avoid taking drastic action. When they raise money, they simply pay down some of the debt, after which they go back to business as usual and run the debt back up again as part of a recurring cycle."

"Fourth" I conclude, "they ain't going to change. They already have a sugar daddy. You'll just be a new one. Why would they give up someone they know for someone they don't know? I just don't see how this works to your advantage or how you can make any return off these guys, much less a big one."

Andrew Scherr then looks over at me and says in a smooth, unemotional voice, "But we'll be majority shareholders. We'll tell them what to do or we'll just get rid of them."

I did not respond. I just let that comment slide. I'm already the skunk at the garden party. No need to make things worse. I glance over at Jeff. He looks pissed off. I continue to feel very badly for him.

Alex Burns looks up from his phone and says to everyone and no one, "Okay. I'm done." He stands up, looks back down at his phone, turns, and speed-walks out of the conference room, narrowly missing the side of the door before heading down the hallway towards his office.

"Well, I guess we're done here," Scherr says. He stands up and walks out the door.

The others get up, collect their unused notepads, and slowly meander out of the room. No handshakes. No "nice to meet you." Nothing. They just get up and leave.

Except for Jeff, who's now giving me one of those mean heat-stares.

"Dude!" he says, looking beyond exasperated with me. "You were not supposed to kill the deal! If we got this deal done, I was going to pocket a huge fee and you were going to get a job!"

Jeff and I have known each other a long time. We can both annoy the crap out of each other. But it never lasts. It's one of those friendships where you forgive a lot. This time I'm on the side needing forgiveness. But one good night of drinking together and bygones will be bygones.

Suddenly, I look at Jeff and say, "Wait! You're getting a fee out of a private equity deal? You're the president of the firm making the investment. How the fuck can that happen?"

Jeff starts to explain when a voice booms from down the hall-way. It's Alex. "JEFF!" He repeats it again: "JEFFREY!"

My friend's face goes from anger to something akin to "Oh, shit."

"Thanks," he finally says. "This will not be fun. Do not leave. I'll be back... hopefully."

A few minutes later, Jeff ambles back into the conference room, gives me an "I don't know what's happening" shrug, and says, "He wants to see you,"

"About what?" I ask.

"'I have no idea. Just go. The little bastard doesn't like to be kept waiting. He has the attention span of a gnat!" he says in a slightly pissed-off voice.

I've pushed all the wrong buttons today, so I'm not looking forward to these next few minutes. I just don't want to say anything that will get Jeff in any hotter water. But I also want—no need—to get paid.

As I'm walking down the hall, everyone seems to be on the phone on the trading desks and in the glass-enclosed offices. No one looks at me. They all seem to have their heads down. Like they're trying to hide from something. It's weird. It's making me even more nervous.

At the far end of the hallway is a huge elbow-shaped office with floor-to- ceiling glass windows. We didn't go by it when Jeff gave me the tour before the meeting. It is Alex Burns' office.

As I get closer to his office, I see something odd. It looks like writing of some sort on all the windows. As I get closer, I can now see that there's magic marker writing, graphs, notes, and all sorts of scribblings covering all the interior windows of Alex's office.

Remember the movie, "A Beautiful Mind," about Nobel Prize winner John Nash? It starred Russell Crowe as Nash. In that movie, Nash is a brilliant but mentally unstable economist and mathematician who teaches Game Theory at Princeton. In the movie, he covers the windows of his living space and office with his notes, thoughts, graphs, and equations. You see it several times over the course of the movie. It's meant to symbolize his unrestrained genius, with the glass representing the invisible barrier between Nash and a great intellectual breakthrough.

Why has Burns replicated this scene? Is he trying to paint himself as some sort of Nobel Prize-worthy genius?

Does he think people haven't seen the movie?

As I near the doorway to the office, still fascinated by the movie parallel, I suddenly spot Burns standing in his office with his arms straight down his side and a wry smile staring at me.

The image in my mind suddenly flips from John Nash in "A Beautiful Mind" to Hannibal Lector in "Silence of the Lambs."

I step into his office and politely ask, "Hi. You want to see me?"

It's then that I notice his office—probably 50 to 75 index cards laid out in meticulous fashion… on the floor!

"What is that?" I ask.

"Oh, those are all the companies I own," he replies casually. "It's how I keep track."

A few moments pass as we both stare at the floor. Neither of us speaks. All I can think of is that the cleaning lady could do serious corporate damage with a vacuum or a broom.

"So, what do you know about wine?" Burns asks me, breaking the silence.

I'm not nervous around him anymore. It dawns on me that he's a kid, and this is all a game to him. So I respond, "I like wine just like me—big, cheap, and white."

Burns giggles like a schoolboy. Then he reaches over onto his desk, grabs an envelope, and hands it to me.

"Here's your check. That was fun today," he says.

"Thank you. If you need additional help, just ask."

"You're friends with Jeff, right? So, he knows how to get ahold of you?"

"Yep, no problem. Thanks again." I turn and make my way out. Walking down the hallway, the trading desks are more thinly staffed than when I'd arrived, I pop my head in Jeff's office and hold up the check.

Jeff is on the phone but puts his hand over it, looks at his watch, and whispers to me, "Connolly's. One hour. On you."

"Deal." I respond and head toward the elevators.

I gotta call my wife.

CHAPTER 14

Connolly's is an Irish bar on 47th and Madison, two and a half or three blocks from Southport's office. There are a few Irish bars in mid-town, and they're all exactly alike.

When I was working up the street and living in a hotel a few days a week, I'd eaten many a late dinner in Connolly's. Like any good Irish bar, it's comfortable, relaxing, and wholly informal. It's Manhattan, so it isn't cheap by the rest of the country's standards. But by Manhattan standards, it's pretty cheap.

Chores done, I stroll into Connolly's about 45 minutes after leaving Southport's office. I grab a seat at the bar and take a deep breath. But I still feel like shit about putting Jeff in a rough spot.

I'm a gin and tonic guy now. When the first one comes, I slug it down. The serving glasses are small, but this is wholly consistent with my drinking style. The first one goes down in three seconds. The second one goes down in three minutes. The third one goes down in 30 minutes, and if there are any after that, they can take forever.

When I was living in Newport, RI, my favorite watering hole was Café Zelda's. It's where I met my wife. It was a great place. Full of sailing bums and all sorts of fascinating people.

My wife was an Assistant Harbor Master in Newport at the time. She's six feet tall. She has short blond hair almost white from the sun, blue eyes, a deep, deep tan, and is just beautiful. Before I'd met her, she'd spent seven straight years working on charter yachts in the Caribbean. The first time I saw her, I was hit by "the thunderbolt."

She told me once that when we first met, she thought I was just another guy with a tall-chick fetish. I mean, she wasn't wrong. But still…

On a busy night when I walked into Zelda's, Bobby the bartender would see me out of the corner of his eye, and then moments later, he'd be holding a pint of Heineken over the heads of the bar crowd. I'd grab it, kill it, and by the time I was done, a second would magically appear above the heads of the crowd. I'd take the second, hand back the dead body of the first, and then work my way through number two.

A few minutes later, I'd catch Bobby's eye, and with a quick nod of recognition between us, number three would be fast approaching. After taking number three, I'd find a vacant spot, sit down, and watch whatever game was on TV.

I've always had a prodigious thirst. When I was little, my mom was worried that I had diabetes. I didn't. I was just thirsty.

So, I'm on number three at Connolly's, looking at my phone, when Jeff walks in and sits two barstools away from me. We're both big guys, so we like a little space between us.

"So, I guess you made an impression today," he starts. He nods to the bartender, whom he knows, or apparently knows him.

"Oban. Rocks," Jeff instructs the bartender, who quickly and professionally pours it and slides it down the bar to Jeff.

"Perfect. Thanks."

I still feel like shit about the meeting, so I immediately launch into a major *mea culpa*.

"Jeff, I'm so sorry. I didn't mean to get you jammed up with Jimmy Fucking Neutron. Maybe I hit the truth button a little too hard in that meeting. I'm so sorry. Who is this fucking kid anyway?" I'm just babbling.

"No, no," Jeff sputters. "That's not what I meant, and who the fuck is Jimmy Neutron?"

"Jimmy Neutron is a cartoon my boys used to watch about a genius middle school kid who bumblefucks his way to saving the world on every show."

Jeff is paying more attention to his drink than to me.

"Anyway, about half an hour after you left," Jeff says, "he walks into my office and says, 'Find a way to hire that guy Bailey.'"

Now, I'm kind of shocked, as I go from thinking I screwed up to being told they want to offer me a job.

"Really?" I squeal. "Are you serious, or are you just fucking with me?"

"No, I'm serious. Burns want to hire you."

"Well, ain't this a day?!" I exclaim. "Hopefully, I'll never see that shithole in New Jersey again. I met Jimmy Neutron for what? Ten minutes? Half the time he was staring at his phone. I've deposited that check, called my wife, and told her I got paid for the first time in a year. And now I might actually get a job at a private equity firm out of this? Damn. I'll have another drink... or ten."

"Not bad, Commodore. Not bad. Now dinner is officially on you," Jeff proclaims.

"Sounds good!" I say.

Secretly, I'm thrilled we're in Connolly's and not The Palm or some other midtown steakhouse, where dinner for the two of us would easily consist of a gallon or more of a fine Italian wine and a couple of steaks the size of Chihuahuas. Such a meal at that kind of place can run well over a grand, no sweat. Eating and drinking with Jeff is fun. Until the bill comes.

"Who's Jimmy Neutron again?" Jeff asks, now more relaxed than when he first walked in.

I give him a quick singing of the "Jimmy Neutron" theme song:

He's a super-powered mind with a mechanical K-9
And he rescues the day from pure de-STRUCT-ion.
This is my theme song... Jimmy Neutron.

Jeff drains his first scotch and laughs. "That's tremendous. Fits Alex perfectly too."

Scotch number two is placed in front of Jeff. He grabs it. Still chuckling as he starts in, "Frankly, I was waiting for Neutron to start giving me shit about Jersey Pharma, but he's fixated on hiring you. He said he mentioned the vineyard to you."

"Vineyard? What vineyard? You guys own a vineyard?" I say in a semi-amused fashion. "He did ask me if I liked wine, and I responded with my usual..."

Jeff cuts me off and says, "Lemme guess: 'big, white, and cheap'?"

I snicker.

"You gotta stop using that line," Jeff says. "And for the record, I've never seen you drink cheap wine. If you recall, you were sitting by yourself, drinking a bottle of Chateau Palmer at the Black Pearl in Newport, when we first met."

"Ssshhh," I butt in, "Don't tell my wife. And it was at the Clarke Cooke House, not the Pearl."

"Whatever, dickhead. Anyway, Neutron—I'm definitely keeping the Neutron thing—everyone in the office will get a kick out of that."

"So," Jeff continues, "Neutron asks me if you would want to run the vineyard on Long Island he bought a few months ago. He paid like $13 million in cash for it and has dumped another $2 to $3 million into it. The guy running it is an absolute moron. Alex hates him, but he has no one else to run it."

"They make wine on Long Island?" I ask. I'm incredulous.

"Yeah, actually there are a ton of vineyards out there. I don't know if they're any good. But little Jimmy Neutron now owns one. Everybody at Southport told him it was a waste of money, but he bought it anyway from some big hedge fund manager he was trying to impress."

"But," I say, "I don't know anything about farming and wine-making. I've run steel and semiconductor companies." A touch of panic is sliding into my voice.

"Well, if you want any more of those paychecks, you're a farmer now. Do me a favor, go see the place. If you think you can do it, I'll bet he'll pay you at least fifteen K a month."

"How much?" I ask.

"Fifteen thousand a month," says Jeff. "It's kind of the starting salary around here."

"I'll go," I say. "I'll go. By the way, two things were a little weird today."

"Only two?" Jeff laughs into his glass.

"Well, at least two. First, what's with you getting a fee for making a private equity investment? I mean, you know just how wrong that is, right?"

"And the second?" Jeff asks.

"Who is this Andrew Scherr? That guy gives me the full-on creeps," I say.

"Ahh. Scherr is Alex's partner. Be very careful with him," Jeff says. "Because Burns hasn't the faintest idea how this business works, Scherr has convinced him that taking a fee is normal in these deals. So, as a result, everyone is just trying to get Alex to agree to a deal so they can get a big fee. Andrew now goes around and says to everyone with a deal, 'I'll help you get Alex to agree to your deal if you split the fee with me.'"

"What the fuck?! That's not only absurd but wrong on so many levels," I say.

"Yes…. and as a result, everyone is trying to rat-fuck everyone else to get a fee. It's ridiculous."

Jeff downs drink number two as number three is plunked down on the bar in front of him.

"Be really careful around Scherr," Jeff repeats. "He's probably the only guy I've ever met who goes into a deal thinking, 'How can I fuck the other guy and get everything for myself?'"

Jeff grabs drink number three.

"Seriously, be careful with all these guys," he adds. "This place is a fucking Pirate Cove."

CHAPTER 15

April 2013

The main house and barn owned by Lieb Cellars in Cutchogue, NY. My mid-week home for five and a half years was surrounded by 22 acres of vineyard.

To get to the east end of Long Island from Boston, you pretty much have no choice but to take the Cross Sound Ferry for the one hour and twenty-minute trip from New London, Connecticut to Orient Point, New York. I'd never taken done that ferry, so as is my habit, I went down the night before and checked into the nearest Hilton. I wanted to be at the vineyard first thing, which apparently means 10:00 am to the staff.

The ferry ride was beautiful. You park your car down below and climb up the stairs to the main passenger area. If you walked to the front of the passenger area and stepped through a small companionway, then lo and behold, there was a nice, tidy little bar area with barstools, tables, and booths.

I could get used to this.

I ordered a gin and tonic and a remarkably good cheeseburger, then sat down at a booth, opened my backpack, and pulled out the financial statements and acquisition documents for the vineyard that had arrived, via FedEx, at my house the previous day.

The first thing anyone and everyone who has ever worked in corporate finance, investment banking, venture capital, or private equity does when handed a new deal is flip to the financial statements. It's reflexive. We all do it. If the financial statements meet your expectations for a possible deal, you read the other bullshit. If they don't, you toss it. Or, if you wish to be polite, you put it down, ignore the document, and pretend you're listening to the presenter tell their story, even though you're not.

This time Southport wasn't paying me to see if this was a good or bad deal in advance of doing it. This was a deal they had already done, and from what Jeff told me the previous week, most people at Southport thought it was a dog. Except of course Jimmy Neutron. So, I wanted to take my time and do my best to see if this place was worth the $12.75 million they paid for it. What did this kid see that everyone else missed?

I took a bite of my cheeseburger and a big swig of my G&T, then pulled out the file and spread the financial statements out on the table.

These financial statements were ugly. Lieb Cellars was a complete disaster. On every dollar of wine they sold, they lost seventy-five cents. There were one, two, three—no, four separate companies involved.

But one thing stuck out right away. One really big thing.

If all this information was correct, Southport had paid $12.75 million for assets worth $6 million. On top of that, the vineyard was losing nearly $750,000 every year. If pitched this deal as an investment, I'd have mentally walked away right then and there, believing that whoever was pitching me must think me an idiot.

If the assets are worth $6.0 million and you paid $12.75 million for them, it stands to reason that you just lost $6.75 and you're going to bleed out another $750,000 per year. Which begs the question: Why would you throw away more than $6 million for the privilege of losing $750,000 a year?

This deal made no sense. But they did it anyway. Why?

There was either something here that Jimmy Neutron knew that I didn't see yet, or this may be the dumbest deal I've ever seen.

Either way, if I agree to run this place, Neutron is going to have to come up with a lot more money to keep it from going under. It's going to take a couple of months to come up with a viable plan to fix it, and another six to twelve months to implement it. So even if all goes right, which it never does, Lieb Cellars is a good two years from standing on its own two feet.

There was one bright spot, though—Premium Wine Group, which made the wine. With 90 percent gross margins, Premium Wine group printed money day in and day out. Lieb was only about 10-15 percent of its business. The rest of their revenue came from about 18 or 19 other vineyards that made their wine there. It was a sweet little business, and the guy who started and ran it knew exactly what he was doing, and it showed. They consistently earned a 20 to 21 percent pre-tax profit.

Prior to the deal with Southport, Premium Wine Group was a separate company. But in what would turn out to be a stroke of good fortune—for me mostly—Southport had combined all four companies under the common ownership of a single company called Premium Wine Acquisitions. And Neutron wanted me to be CEO of Premium Wine Acquisitions.

That opened all sorts of safety valves for an operator like me. If I agreed to run this place, Premium Wine Group's cash flow would be under my control. That means in a pinch, it could help cover the costs from a money-losing dog like Lieb Cellars for a year or two while I was turning it around.

Southport had paid all cash for the business. There were no bank loans, which means there are no bank-imposed covenants prohibiting related company transfers. All the shareholders owned varying amounts of the same assets. So, no conflicts of interests there, and with Southport owning 92 percent, I had only one person to please—Jimmy Neutron.

The trick, however, would be to not kill the goose that laid the golden egg. That could make things messy all around, especially for me.

If the whole place went under, it would be a wet dream for a creditor's attorney. With a billion-dollar private equity firm and a hugely successful hedge fund manager as owners and potential defendants, it would take their awfully expensive attorneys about 30 seconds to pin all the blame on me as a "rogue" manager. So, I had to be incredibly careful, and I'd need a fallback plan in case something went wrong.

Still, a lot of things bothered me about this deal, so I started to jot them down.

First, there were a lot of inter-company revenues. That means that companies under the same ownership were generating revenue on their books by selling their products and services to the other companies under the same ownership. In fact, two of these companies were deriving 100 percent of their revenue from the others. This type of activity is common in big companies and conglomerates, but in a small company with a less sophisticated accounting staff, it's a recipe for problems.

Ultimately, all inter-company revenues are supposed to be eliminated when the companies consolidate all their financial statements. But in little companies, sometimes that consolidation doesn't happen. I was worried about that here.

It went like this. Lieb Vines owned the grapevines and was paid a fee by Lieb Vineyards, who grew the grapes, which they sold to Premium Wine Group, who turned the grapes into wine, which they then sold to Lieb Cellars, who sold the wine to whoever wanted to buy and hopefully drink it.

So ultimately, that meant that Lieb Cellars had to sell enough wine each year to pay Premium Wine Group to make the wine, Lieb Vineyards to grow the grapes, and Lieb Vines for the privilege of using the vines.

It was far too complicated. For little companies like this, such complications can kill.

I now wanted to examine the closing documents. Specifically, I wanted to know what the buyer's obligations were to the sellers, and what the sellers' obligations to the buyer were now that the deal was done.

As I pulled that part of the package out of the FedEx envelope, my initial reaction was that I had my hands on an exhibit, not the actual acquisition document. A merger or acquisition document can run into the hundreds of pages.

This felt like I had my hands on a high school term paper.

I open the envelope and take out the folder. There were three separate documents, each only about ten pages, including the signature page. Not a whole lot of paper to transfer 48 acres, four businesses, over 30,000 square feet of commercial and industrial space, and an 8,000 square-foot home with a built-in pool and a 5,000 square foot barn with space for four cars and two apartments in exchange for $12.75 million in cash. I've worked with lawyers who needed more pages than that just to get through the definitions.

I immediately pull out my yellow highlighter, my red felt tip pen, and my blue ball point. I had just under an hour before we docked on the other side of Long Island Sound, so I went to work.

In my first read, I'm just trying to highlight main points in yellow.

My second read-through essentially focuses on things that could seem problematic or subjects about which I need more information. They get highlighted in red.

My third and final read-through has to do with things that just seem like a problem. They get circled in blue.

After three quick reads, one paragraph is highlighted in yellow, underlined in red, and circled in blue. It's on page four.

Under Section 5—Representations and Warranties. I find this head-spinner. Paragraph C (vi) states, *"The Purchaser and Seller acknowledge and accept that the other party to the transaction may have material non-public information about the Company that they do not have, and which has not been disclosed."*

In other words, the seller is saying to the buyer that the seller may not have told the buyer all the bad stuff about the company. Or, that they may not even know if more bad stuff exists. And if they don't know about it, then they certainly can't tell the buyer about it, so the buyer will just have to find out about it on their own and deal with the consequences.

Then C (vii) goes on to say essentially: *"If something really bad happened during the time we owned the company and we didn't tell you, well, it's your problem, not ours."*

How did this get by Southport's attorney? Did they even read this document?

As the ferry is pulling into Orient Point, Long Island, and I hop in my car, I can't stop thinking: "Whoever did this deal at Southport is an idiot."

But the sellers? They got the deal of the century.

CHAPTER 16

Every time I start a new gig working at a distressed company, I prepare myself for the unexpected. Leaping into the unknown is kind of a thrill to me. Every company I go to is a mystery when I get there, and I love solving a good mystery. It forces you to question and learn. That's my idea of fun.

While all struggling companies are completely different, they all share similar characteristics. Most companies wind up in trouble due to one or a series of bad decisions.

My job is to figure out what those decisions were, who made them, why they made them, and if they can be reversed, because not all broken companies can be fixed. Some must be allowed to die.

In what I call my "3GP" analysis, a successful turnaround of a fixable company depends on learning a few things.

First, do they make a good product? Do they make a product or service that someone (or preferably everyone) wants to buy? If not, then they're done. There's no need for them to survive. If Lieb is making shitty wine, then there's not much anyone can do to help them. If, on the other hand, they're making wine that people enjoy, they may have a future.

Second, do they have a good staff? Do they have the right people in the right jobs? Do they have decent-quality management? In Lieb's case, you had an absentee owner more focused (and rightfully so) on his hedge fund. Lieb Cellars was Alex's hobby. It was a company he paid minimal attention to and hired people to run it for him. Did he have the right people running it? The place had never made money, so I'm thinking no.

Making money is the report card for any manager. If you have a good product, a rich hedge fund owner willing to support you, and are still losing money, then you get a big fat "F" on your report card. Chances are you're just there for the paycheck, or until the rich owner tires of your performance.

As my grandmother used to say—I've seen the wisdom in her snide remark over and over, "The fish stinks from the head."

Finally, good process. What do their internal decision-making processes look like? A well-defined management process with regular planning, monitoring, and oversight can make a bad manager look better and a good manager look great. Oversight, communications, and accountability are everything when running a company. Are big decisions made after contemplation and discussion? Or are decisions made on the fly while passing someone in the hallway? All successful companies have structure. Ones that don't will never live up to their potential.

So, do they have a good product? Some think so.

Is their management capable? Well, the company has been around for almost 25 years, and it has never made money. So, I'd say no.

Do they have good internal processes? I'd quickly learn that they had no processes whatsoever.

I'm a decent manager, not a great one. But I can assess people very quickly and figure out their strengths and weakness. I'm also a process junkie. If Lieb has a good product and I can find the right manager, then with the aid of some process and structure, this company may have a shot.

My high school football coach once assessed me this way: "You're not fast on your feet, but you can see the whole field." That's a nice way of saying I'm a big picture guy.

My first impression of Lieb Cellars? I was decidedly unimpressed. I remember sitting in the tasting room the first time I visited, interviewing all the managers one by one, except the CFO. The CFO was a part-timer and nowhere to be found. Everyone had been informed by Southport that I'd be there on Tuesday morning. The CFO didn't call and didn't reschedule. She made no contact. Strike one against the CFO.

Everyone else was there. The general manager, the director of operations, and Peter, the marketing consultant who, it seemed, was incapable of shutting up.

As I sat down alone with each, I thanked them for their time and described a little bit about my background. I didn't mention to anyone that I'd been hired to oversee the entire operation, including Premium Wine Group. I didn't want anyone to feel threatened. I made it sound as if I was there to study the place, which had the added benefit of being true. My goal for these meetings was to inspire as much candor as possible.

I started with Peter, the talkative consultant. He knew why I was there because he was paid directly by Southport. He lives in Manhattan and apparently chums around with Alex Burns. Or at least claims he does. So, I donned kid gloves for him. When I asked Peter what needed to happen to make this place run better, he basically did a commercial for himself.

He talked about his many years of restaurant ownership in Manhattan, his years as a brand manager for Grey Goose Vodka, and how he was tight with Malcolm Gosling, the head of the family which owns Goslings Rum of Bermuda. If half of what he said was true, he could be helpful because I knew nothing about the alcohol business.

But the guy could talk a blue streak, and none of it was in a straight line. If he was trying to add context, he never came back to what he was adding context to. A meaningful conversation with him required a lot of rhetorical whittling by me.

Next came Sarah, the Director of Operations. She was cool and cerebral and gave considered answers to my questions. She had been there for quite a few years and was clearly the institutional memory of the place. When I needed an explanation as to why something had happened, Sarah had the answer. I could tell that there was a lot she wasn't telling me, though. She was too smart to be completely candid. Not on the first meeting.

Then there was Gary, the General Manager. Now he was a piece of work. Over the years, I've always asked variations of the same three questions at these initial meetings;

First, if you had an unlimited checkbook, what would you change to make this company better?

Second, if this company went out of business, would any-body—outside of the employees—miss it?

Third, what wakes you up at night about this place?

When asked what he would change, he answered that he would *"make everybody listen to him."*

He also said no one would miss the company if it went out of business. In all the years I've asked these questions, Gary is the only one who answered this way.

Truly remarkable.

After a couple of hours, I thanked everyone and told them I was going to make my way over to Premium Wine Group.

Lieb Cellars was in sad shape. Everybody was in charge and nobody was in charge.

On my drive over to Premium, I was wondering if Gary was right.

CHAPTER 17

Premium Wine Group is an industrial-sized wine-making facility. Known in the industry as a "custom crush," it's the largest and most modern custom crush east of the Mississippi River.

Whereas everything at Lieb Cellars was underwhelming, everything at Premium Wine Group was impressive. Capable of making 238,000 gallons (1.2 million bottles or 100,000 cases) of wine at any one time, everything about it was well thought-out. While they did make the wine for Lieb, they also made it for 18 or 19 other members of the industry.

The important thing to know about a custom crush is that they don't sell wine. They make it for others. They don't own a single vine nor a single grape. They buy no bottles or labels. It's a brilliant business model. They simply charge their customers for use of their winemaking and bottling facilities.

A custom crush customer is generally a vineyard that grows grapes and sells their wine to the public. But many vineyards don't make or bottle their own wine. That's because the equipment is so expensive, and because turning grapes into wine is a highly technical and complex process. It's both science and art.

That's where the custom crush comes in. At harvest time, customers deliver their grapes to Premium Wine Group. Once there, they're pressed, crushed, and de-stemmed on the crush pad. Then the juice is pumped into one of over 100 big aluminum tanks at Premium.

Once in the tank, the winemaking process, which can take between 90 days for whites and rosé to several years for reds, begins. When it's ready to be either transferred to a barrel or bottled, Premium does that as well. Once bottled, the vineyard either picks it up themselves or sends it to a warehouse somewhere pending sale. Or it stays on the premises and racks up monthly storage charges.

Every time someone at Premium touches the wine, there's a fee.

You receive the grapes in at harvest? Bill it.

Crush it? Bill it.

Pump it over to a tank? Bill it.

Let it age in the tank? Bill it … every month.

Add sugar or other ingredients? Upcharge them for the ingredients and bill it.

Chemical testing? Bill it.

Age it on-site? Again, bill it every month.

Bottling? Bill it.

Store the finished wine on-site? Bill it some more.

That's how you get a business with 90 percent gross margins. All you're really on the hook for is payroll and utilities. It's one of the best business models I've ever seen.

Over at Premium Wine Group, I met Russell, the affable Australian genius who founded Premium in 2000 and sold it to Southport. The moment I walked into the tank room, I quickly appreciated the scale of the operation, looked at him, and said, "Now this is a business."

Russell was the smartest guy in the Long Island wine industry, and everyone knew it. He was also the humblest—an odd trait for an Australian, at least in my experience.

CHAPTER 18

Lieb Cellars
Cutchogue, NY
May 2013

The conference room at Lieb Cellars is also the wine library room. It's a well-appointed room located at the rear of the tasting room of the main building in Cutchogue, New York. Artwork and full racks of Lieb Wine tastefully cover the walls. On most days, you can find customers sitting there, enjoying a glass of wine with friends. Some days, there are formal wine tastings going on or even wine education classes.

But until noon each day, it's a workspace. A conference room.

It seems the only person Southport told I was taking over as CEO was Peter. But he didn't seem to understand or, as was most likely the case, not paying attention. He somehow believed I was there as a "compliance guy." Someone whose job it was to make sure nobody did anything stupid. I guess he wasn't too far off. But because of his close relationship with Alex Burns, he thought I had no oversight over him.

Boy, was he wrong!

I never announced I was in charge. But it should have been crystal clear when I conducted my first managers' meeting. I was in charge. And I made it clear that these meetings would happen every single week for the entirety of my time there. Which they did.

Running a weekly meeting forces people to be accountable. It makes people explain their roles and responsibilities. It also allows them to point a spotlight on where they shine as well as ask for help when they need it.

I take copious notes at these meetings. Usually in a hardcover notebook. That way I can remember and revisit the promises and progress made. Or lost.

Gary, Peter, and Sarah were present for that initial meeting. The CFO? She was too busy with her other clients. That was really not sitting well with me. I had no idea what the accounting looked like. How much cash was in the bank? What was the cash flow situation in either the near or distant future? I didn't know. I was flying blind.

Strike two.

I began the meeting by informing the managers that these meetings would occur each week. I also stressed that they better have a damn good reason for missing one.

It was at this regular weekly meeting that we were going to set and measure our short- and long-term goals and collectively solve our problems. At these meetings, I emphasized, everything would be on the table. No question would be out of line, with the goal of achieving full transparency among the managers. We all needed to know our goals and how we were reaching them.

I went first, and since I was new, I'd ask a few simple questions. First, with the busy summer season right around the corner, was the place ready? What did it need to make the most out of the all-important summer season? Are we properly staffed? Do we have the right amount of inventory?

Before anyone could answer, Gary jumped in and said, "We have one problem that we need to discuss."

"And that is…?" I replied.

"We don't have enough money to cover payroll this week," he said.

"Excuse me?" I said.

Gary now has my full and undivided attention. This is my second day here, and already we're going to miss payroll?

Lovely.

"If you we don't get money in like today or tomorrow, we're going to miss payroll on Friday. Today is Tuesday," Gary observed.

"I know what day it is," I said, probably failing to not sound peeved. "But why are you telling me this? Where's our CFO, whom

I've yet to meet, and why is she not here at our first staff meeting to tell me this herself?"

"Our CFO is part-time. She only works Tuesday and Thursday," Sarah chimed in.

"And if I'm not mistaken, isn't today in fact Tuesday? So, where is she?" I ask.

"She won't be in until the end of the day. She has a lot of other clients." I get the sense that Sarah is one of those quiet bomb-throwers who loves to roll a grenade into a conversation.

Is she testing me? She better not be. I got Irish Alzheimer's. For those of you who don't know, Irish Alzheimer's is where you forget everything but a grudge. So the CFO's messing with me would be bad for her.

"And how much do we pay our mysterious CFO?" I ask. My sarcasm is now on full display.

"Well, she bills by the hour, but it usually comes out to be between eight and ten thousand a month," Sarah says.

"Great deal for her! Would you be kind enough to ask her to come in and introduce herself to me? That is, if it isn't too much of an inconvenience to her?" I ask Sarah.

"No problem" she says.

I like Sarah. She's a strong lady who doesn't give a shit what people think of her. But I'm not sure I trust her. Because she doesn't give a shit what people think of her.

"This is all fine and good," says Gary, "but what are we going to do about payroll? People have bills to pay!" Gary is whining. I'm quickly tiring of him.

See, Gary brings up problems but doesn't offer solutions. And you know what that means: He's not a problem-solver. If you can't solve problems, you have no business being in charge.

Peter bides his time before weighing in.

"Hey... I don't want to interrupt," Peter says, having found his moment to interject. He's speaking at a fast and furious space.

"Do you want me to call Alex and have him wire money in for payroll? Burnsey and I are best friends. We hang out a lot on the weekends in the city. I'll tell you a story. A few weeks ago, we were sitting in a bar having drinks when he decided to go buy a painting.

He got up and said he would be right back. Half an hour later, he came with a receipt from the art dealer down the street. He showed it to us. He paid almost a million dollars and put it on his credit card. Alex and I, we're like best friends."

"For the record, and so I'm clear, what is your job here again?" I ask.

"Oh. I work for Alex. I report to him," Peter says.

That was news to me, especially since Alex made a point of telling Jeff, who told me the exact opposite. But I give Peter credit. If he's trying a power play at our first staff meeting, he's got balls. But in my mind, he's now also a problem.

Gary jumps back into the conversation. He's tired of listening to Peter, and it's quickly becoming clear they do not get along.

"Listen, what are we going to do about payroll?" Gary again asks.

Turning to Sarah, I ask, "Is payroll generally a problem here?"

"It has been in the past," she says in a very professional, matter-of-fact fashion.

"So, what do you usually do?" I ask.

"I call the owner and he wires in the money," says Sarah.

"Really?" I say. "Just a phone call?"

I'm troubled by this casual sloshing around of money. There's clearly no cash plan in this joint. In fact, I doubt there's any plan about anything. These folks are making things up as they go.

Peter then steps on my line of questioning in a way that pisses me off.

"If you want me to bail you out on this, let me know, and I'll call Burnsey. No skin off my back. I don't get paid here anyway. I get paid by Southport. Let me call him," he says in an almost stream-of-consciousness boast.

"No! You'll not call anyone about this without my permission!"

The last thing I need is this unguided missile calling Southport and undercutting me.

"But what about payroll? We need the money by tomorrow!" Gary pleads.

"Relax. No one is missing payroll on my watch," I say quietly, nearly hissing through clenched teeth.

I turn to Sarah, who has a bit of a smirk on her face—I suspect she's enjoying this—and say politely, "Put an ad in whatever paper you have out here. We need a new CFO. Immediately."

My first staff meeting isn't going well. So I end it.

As I start to get up to leave the room, Peter seems to want my attention. I don't think he realizes this isn't a smart move at this moment. My first managers' meeting has been a disaster. But Peter does not read social cues. At least not the obvious anger-based ones I'm throwing off.

"While I've got you here, I want to run something by you," he says.

"Ok, what's up?" I respond, trying not to appear pissed off.

"So, you know, ever since Southport took over here, people have been a little nervous about stuff," he says. It's a fair enough comment, and it comes up in almost every one of my engagements. So, I relax a little.

"About what?" I soften.

"Just general stuff. You know, lots of stress about jobs, the future … you know."

"Let me guess: You have an idea on how to ease that stress?" I respond.

"Yeah. Listen to this...." Peter says as he reanimates before my eyes.

"What if we took this room and turn it into a game room? You know, put a Foosball table in here. Maybe a big screen TV too. You know, employees could come in here and burn off a little steam. Kind of like they have at Facebook! Whaddya think?"

"But don't we use this as a conference room, and don't paying customers sit in here and drink wine? What about that? This room generates revenue!" I say. I'm perplexed. I don't understand the thinking behind the question. But now I'm starting to get really pissed by his sheer cluelessness.

"Yeah, but you know, this is a lifestyle business," he says.

Stunned by the stupidity of the idea, I fire back, "Yeah, for the customer, you moron!"

Not my finest moment. I apologized the next week.

We covered payroll no problem. I wired in the deficit from my personal account.

On my watch, all my employees got paid, in full and on time... except me.

I didn't tell my wife.

CHAPTER 19

Cutchogue, NY

I never did meet the old CFO—only her bookkeeper, whom she sent over twice a week. The bookkeeper was a perfectly nice and competent person.

Her boss? Who knows? A ghost and, as we would soon learn, an incompetent one at that.

I once called the CFO and asked her for the checking account balance. She asked, "The bank balance or the book balance?"

I was taken aback by the question and immediately wondered if the account might be overdrawn, and that she might be playing with the float. It's something we all have done, but it often does not end well, so I muttered, "Both."

She then proceeded to explain to me that, "you know, when you write a check, the bank doesn't know you have written it until it's presented for payment. That could take several days. So, there's a difference between the bank balance and the book balance."

I was floored. Here I'm 55 years old. I've run companies with over $100 million in revenues. I've actively managed tens of millions at the seventh-largest bank in North America. Now I'm being spoken to as if I'm a 12-year-old with his first checking account.

Fortunately, I was heading into Southport's offices the next day to interview her replacement, whom I hired in about ten minutes.

CHAPTER 20

Cutchogue, NY
July 2013

Dave Sanatore, the new CFO, was a godsend. He was thorough, dedicated and, like all good CFOs, a pain in the ass at times. I mean that in a good way.

He didn't brook shortcuts. He believed in the beauty of process. He wasn't a degreed accountant or CPA, which was fine with me. Hell, I was a political science major and got my MA in corporate communications, so I'm not one to harp on having the perfect degree. But he was tenacious and, when given a task, would work overtime to get it done well and on time.

Dave was my first hire. But Ami Opisso was both my second and my best.

In late May, Gary was let go, and Peter introduced me to Ami. A native of Long Island wine country, she had worked on liquor accounts at big Chicago and New York advertising agencies. She'd fallen in love with vineyard life, gotten married, left New York City, and moved back to her hometown to make a life for herself and eventually start a family.

The first time I met her, one thing stood out right away: She was smart as a whip. The second thing was that she was tough. How did I know that? She negotiated her pay like a pro.

I look for a specific type when I'm hiring. Like any corporate finance person, I've made hundreds of presentations to rooms full of very smart financiers, lawyers, investors, and investment bankers. They can be a brutal bunch, and there's always one person who wants to prove they're smarter than the presenter.

People who can step into a room like that, make a presentation, answer difficult questions with confidence, and get a tough, skeptical room to support them can be described in one word I like—"streetable."

In other words, you could put them in front of a hostile Wall Street crowd to make a presentation, and they would be fine. More important, so would you.

It takes smarts, toughness, and confidence. Ami had all three.

What I was looking for—what Lieb Cellars needed—were streetable people. That was a big ask for the North Fork of Long Island, which is rural, farmy, and artsy.

There are also a lot of retirees. The North Fork is the antithesis of its glamorous, glitzy, and oh-so-posh cousin to the south—the world-famous "Hamptons." In short, the talent pool of streetable people on the North Fork was pretty darn shallow.

With Dave and Ami, I lucked out.

Ami was initially hired to be the Manager of Production, but it soon became apparent to me that everyone naturally gravitated to her to answer their questions. With authentic poise, she easily stepped into and filled any and every void that existed in the day-to-day operations of Lieb Cellars.

Believe me, there were many. By the end of the year, I'd make her General Manager.

Quick funny story: One day Ami and I were driving to the South Fork to look at Lieb's new and as yet unopened tasting room in East Hampton.

We were in my car on the Shelter Island Ferry going from Greenport to the North Ferry Dock on Shelter Island. It was on that ten-minute ferry ride that I asked Ami if she would be interested in being General Manager of Lieb Cellars.

Her response was amazing. First, she answered, "Yes." Then she said, "But I have one problem."

I paused and let her catch her breath. "I'm pregnant," she said.

I chuckled and said, "I don't care. We'll work around that. You're the right person for the job."

Ami wasn't big on showing emotions. But she leaned over and gave me a hug, thanked me, and then made me promise I'd not tell a soul about her pregnancy.

Listen, I have two kids. I understand that whole first trimester thing. I also understand that breaking that secret can make smart, rational people crazy.

Me? Late on New Year's Eve 1994, I blurted out that my wife was pregnant. I was three sheets to the wind. That's why I let it slip.

Learned that lesson the hard way. Telling someone you're going to have a baby is a huge deal. I told Ami her secret was safe with me.

I never told a soul. Except my wife, Chris.

With Dave and Ami in place, I now had a decent management team. As a result, I whittled down the weekly meetings to Ami, Russell the winemaker, Dave, and me. This would be the core management team that would run the show. Each one of us was confident of our abilities and eminently streetable. It was a solid team who would be put to a variety of very difficult tests.

CHAPTER 21

July 2013

It's difficult to describe just how chaotic and disorganized the financial records at Lieb were at the time. When I got there in May, Southport had two accounting firms on site trying to get some sort of clarity on the financial situation. But to do so, they had to recreate a paper trail for thousands of transactions which had incomplete or in many cases no corresponding records.

Imagine finding hundreds of financial transactions in the bank statements with no corresponding paperwork. It was that bad.

Southport's plan was to merge the vineyard entities into a publicly-traded shell corporation. This type of transaction is called a "reverse merger." It's a simple concept. Find a publicly-traded company with no operating business and acquire an operating business using the publicly traded shares as the purchase price. Once the transaction is complete, the operating business is now a publicly-traded company, complete with a stock price quoted on one of the many publicly-traded exchanges.

This brings certain advantages. As a public company, your stock is a currency with which you can raise more money to expand, acquire another business, or raise operating capital to fund your losses.

It also brings disadvantages. The cost of being a publicly-traded company can be very high—running into the millions of dollars per year. This is a cost smaller companies simply can't afford. Part of that cost is having audited financials.

Having audited financial statements means an independent outside firm—in this case, McGladrey (now RSM)—comes in, reviews your financial statements, and conducts varying tests of inventory, accounts receivable, accounts payable, and a host of other items.

If you pass all the tests, they issue an "opinion," which states that in their professional estimation, the "company's financial statements are fairly and appropriately presented, without any identified exceptions, and in compliance with generally accepted accounting principles (GAAP)."

In sum, the auditor thinks the company's financial statements are reliable.

But nothing about Lieb's internal finances was reliable. In fact, the financial records of this company were poster children for unreliability.

Dave, our new CFO, came to me one day with a statement from a vendor marked "PAID IN FULL" in big bold red letters.

But there was a problem.

Dave, being the very thorough guy he is, could find no record of any check, wire transfer, ACH, or other type of payment to this vendor in the amount given in the statement.

Nothing.

Not only is Dave a thorough guy, but he's also worrier, and when he worries, he talks… incessantly and without stopping.

After I calm him down, he shows me the statement. It's from Nationwide, our insurance provider, and shows that we have paid $75,056.55 so far in 2013.

But here's the problem: Neither Lieb Cellars nor Premium Wine Group, nor any other of the companies involved, have any record of paying Nationwide anything.

To make matters worse, Dave keeps running across the same problem with other vendors.

Being a smart guy, Dave concludes—correctly, I might add— that there must be another checking account somewhere and that the bills must be getting paid out of that account. We just had to find it.

Then it occurs to me. I'd already moved the Lieb and Premium Wine Group checking accounts to the Bank of America branch in Southold, the town next to Cutchogue. I personally approve every check written on those Bank of America accounts.

But... the wire transfer for my consulting fees from Southport were paid out of an account at First Republic Bank in New York City. The only thing I've been working on for Southport is the vineyard. Could there be another vineyard account I don't know about? And if I don't know about it, do McGladrey and the other accounting firm know about it?

See, in the post-Enron era, transparency and full disclosure are concepts and bywords on everybody's minds and lips. Arthur Anderson & Co, founded in 1913, employed 28,000 people. But when it was convicted alongside Enron in 2001, it surrendered its license to practice as a certified public accountant in 2002.

All but a handful of Arthur Anderson's 28,000 employees immediately lost their jobs. Enron and Arthur Anderson became a cautionary tale writ large for business guys like me.

Even worse, no CPA firm wanted to be the next Arthur Anderson.

In 2002, the Enron-Arthur Anderson debacle was the catalyst for the landmark Sarbanes-Oxley Act. As a result, withholding material information from your auditors could now be prosecuted as a felony. Committing financial statement fraud could bring on monetary penalties imposed by the SEC and Department of Justice, as well as non-monetary sanctions such as censures, trading suspensions and, as it did with Enron, jail time for the executives in charge.

Now, Southport has two attorneys working on staff full-time. To cover my ass, I call one of them and ask if there's an additional checking account, and if there is, I need the bank statements for the auditors.

Within a few hours, I hit the jackpot. There *was* another account, and they were sending me the bank statements.

Daniel ████████ <████████@southportlane.com>
Mon, Aug 5, 2013, 7:23 PM
to me, Darren, Alexander

Richard, I'm sending you all of the bank statements that I have starting in February. I don't think the accounts had very much activity before then since we were not operating the Premium businesses. I'll ask Darren for the remaining bank statements, if any.

Please wait for authorization from Alex before releasing to McGladrey.

--

Daniel ███████████ | Assistant General Counsel
Southport Lane
350 Madison Avenue, 21st Floor | New York, NY 10017
Tel: (212) 729-3247 | Direct: (212) 729-1335
www.SouthportLane.com

***

I did find curious the admonition not to show the statements to McGladrey, PWA's auditors, without Alex Burns' authorization. But maybe Daniel was just being super cautious.

The very next day, I received all of the bank statements from First Republic Bank going back to when the account was opened in October 2012.

I was not prepared for what they would reveal.

CHAPTER 22

Home
August 6, 2013

During my time as CEO of the companies on Long Island, I usually worked from home on Mondays and Fridays, head down to the ferry for the trip to Lieb on either Monday night or Tuesday morning, then come back home Thursday nights.

To be honest, this was also pretty self-serving. You see, my son Reid was playing freshman high school football. The freshman games were played on Monday afternoons. The varsity games were on Friday nights. Throughout those years, I never missed a game of his.

I always felt a little guilty about this, so I started working early Saturday mornings to make up for it. Over the course of the next five years, there was always something I was worried about or that demanded my attention. As a result, many Saturday mornings often turned into full ten-hour workdays.

***

It was a typical August day. We live in a beachy town, so the weather is always a little cooler than a few miles inland or in Boston. My wife would be out in the gardens. My two sons had summer jobs. So, I had the opportunity to spend a few hours on this week's vineyard problem.

I figured the best way to organize it was to take every transaction on the bank statements Daniel had sent me and enter them into a QuickBooks file. Not very exciting work. But at least I could organize things.

I figured that after I was done, Christina and I'd probably go down to the *haa-ba*—where they dock boats. This is suburban Boston, after all. We'll have a drink and maybe dinner in one of the harbor front restaurants.

That was how we spent the occasional summer Saturdays now that I was earning a paycheck again. Nothing expensive. A cheap date night. She didn't mind.

Christina had lived on charter yachts in the Caribbean and Maine for seven years. She was almost always the only girl on the yacht. So, she had seen guys at their worst.

Nothing my sons or I could do could faze her. I've said for years… she's the ultimate low-maintenance unit. For me, it doesn't get better than her.

***

To start my task, I printed the bank statements that Daniel had e-mailed to me. I had them all (still do).

I wasn't ready for what came next.

Let me start at the beginning. The account was opened on October 2, 2012. On October 3, 2012, three separate wire transfer deposits from Southport Lane, each in the identical sum of $6,060,000 for a total of $18,018,000, were credited to the account.

Then, the very next day, $3,000,000 got wired out to Southport Specialty Finance, and another $10,775,000 was wired to the law firm representing the seller of the vineyard properties.

The money for the vineyard purchase makes sense—well, it made sense from a money movement perspective. But for an accurate assessment of the price for the vineyard, it made no sense.

The $3,000,000 to Southport Specialty Finance got my special attention, though.

I plugged in a few more transactions from the bank statements. As I recorded entry after entry, my concern continued to grow.

What I found was, um… worrisome to say the least.

Hmm… TD Ameritrade, AFI Capital, Merrill Lynch? Seems pretty clear that someone was tucking some money into their brokerage accounts.

But Raubritter LLC? That one raised eyebrows. It looked German. Does Southport or the vineyard have a relationship in Germany? Who knows? But a quick trip to Google Translate gave me a hint that this had nothing to do with the vineyard.

Turns out, Raubritter in German means "Robber Baron." That took a while to sink in. Who would name their company that? And why?

Done with the October 2012 statement, I grabbed the one for November 2012. The beginning balance on November 1, 2012, was $3,924,825. There were only two entries for that month. A monthly consulting check to someone who added not one whit of value to the vineyard. And another check for $350,000 made out to Foster Jennings Inc.

Jeff had told me a little about Foster Jennings. It was an insurance company in Oklahoma which Andrew Scherr, along with a guy named Scott Hartman, were trying to gain control of. But why take the money from an account set up for the benefit of the wine companies? The list of questionable transactions was growing.

For the accounting geeks out there, I'm not an accountant, but over the years I've internalized Generally Accepted Accounting Principles at the 50,000-foot level, so I recorded these and the wire to Southport Specialty Finance in the QuickBooks file as Transaction Expenses. But to be honest, I had no idea whether that was right.

It isn't uncommon for investment firms to pay themselves some sort of fee to cover out-of-pocket and transactional expenses (lawyers' and accountants' fees, for example). But $3,650,000 out of $18,018,000 equals 20.21 percent. A usual fee is somewhere between 2 percent and 10 percent. This was out of the ordinary. And if Southport was truly managing over $1 billion, as it advertised, why ransack this relatively small account?

Having been at the vineyard now for three months, I thought I knew the names of all the players, all the vendors, all the consultants. You know, the members of the financial ecosystem any company needs to move forward and be successful. But Southport Specialty Finance, Raubritter, Foster Jennings, some brokerage accounts? These were outliers. They didn't fit neatly into any proper category.

Then it occurs to me: What are the auditors going to say when I spring this on them?

But I'm really wondering why they deposited $18 million in an account for Premium Wine Acquisition, only to wire it out to unrelated entities right away. They controlled the cash. They managed over $1 billion. Why didn't they wire into the vineyard account only that which would be used to buy the vineyard? Why move the money in, only to move almost 20 percent of it out in such a short time?

When I worked in the investment arm of a big bank, I'd been forced to take anti-money laundering courses. In fact, I used to joke—still do—that I'm a certified money launderer.

My suspicious nature told me that this was odd. But my more rational self told me there was probably a logical explanation. I just didn't know what it was.

All these wire transfers flying out moments after they came in were going to be a problem, especially for me when I brought up the subject.

The only transfer of funds in October 2012 that made sense to me was $10,775,000 to the attorney representing the seller of the vineyard. But even that seemed odd. The transfer documents I read on the ferry on my first trip over back in April evidenced a sale price of $12,750,000. More troubling, the closing didn't happen until February 2013. So why did they wire 85 percent of the purchase price to the sellers' counsel four months before the closing?

Money sloshing around always raises eyebrows. Don't get me wrong. I've done it and learned the hard way to regret it.

But if you must do it to survive, you better have your best lawyer and accountant create an unassailable paper trail. Because if you don't and the company goes under, creditors' attorneys will make you look like the second coming of Bernie Madoff and Charles Ponzi in a heartbeat.

A good lawyer or a shitty lawyer, it doesn't matter. Either will pin everything on you personally. You may have only transferred $100. But they will make it sound like you filched a million and blew it all on cocaine and hookers in Vegas.

The truth is irrelevant to them. The only thing that matters is what they can get a judge or jury to believe, or whatever they can get the defendant(s) to cough up to settle the dispute.

To make matters worse, the relationship between the audit prep firm, McGladrey, and Southport Lane was deteriorating rapidly. I was stuck smack dab in the middle of that one.

A few weeks earlier, Bruce Bernstein, the engagement manager for McGladrey, and I began a series of frank conversations about the state of the accounting records at Lieb Cellars. Or more accurately, the lack thereof. After four months of work, the audit prep firm had billed over $200,000 for what they believed would be a two-week engagement. McGladrey itself had billed over $50,000, and the end to this effort was nowhere in sight.

Sitting in the office at the Lieb Cellars house, Bernstein basically told me one afternoon that getting a "clean" opinion on the reliability of Lieb Cellars' financial statements was, in his professional opinion, becoming questionable. From what I'd seen up to that point, he was right. I couldn't say that, though.

Alex Burns and Andrew Scherr, on the other hand, wanted the audited statements now. They began staking out the position—to me—that if it was taking this long, then the audit prep firm and the audit firm were just riding the clock, trying to take advantage of Southport by creating a massive billing event. On occasion, Alex would call me up screaming.

Andrew? He's too controlled, too sophisticated. By what he says, he indirectly threatens your job. He makes it known that they might decide to shut down the vineyard, leaving unsaid the obvious: I'd be out of a job. Andrew was smart and he was smooth.

The truth was that the audit team at McGladrey was right. The vineyard deal was just ugly. Hugely over-priced. Shitty documentation. Terrible execution. Little or no due diligence. Accounting that was not only wrong but, in many places, non-existent.

Then, amid all this consternation, we had this phantom bank account with a shitload of problematic transactions.

There was no way this ended smoothly or cheaply.

CHAPTER 23

August 13, 2013
Southport Lane's Office
350 Madison Ave.
New York City

On Monday night, August 12, I was summoned to Manhattan, not by Alex but by his assistant, Loren. Nice girl. Pretty efficient. I made it a point to stay on her good side. It was clear Alex relied heavily on her.

My first job out of college in 1980 was as an Assistant to the Mayor of New Haven, CT. When I first started on the job, I was told by several people that you don't cross Angela, the Mayor's Executive Assistant. "Angela can help you, and she can hurt you. So be nice to her. Keep her on your side, and don't squander your opportunities with her." I made a pledge to myself to do the same with Loren.

Loren gave no reason or agenda for the meeting the next day. Just that Alex wants to see me at 11:00 am tomorrow and that we will be meeting in the large conference room.

So I spent the rest of the afternoon converting all of the First Republic Bank statements to a QuickBooks file, told my wife I'd been summoned, made hotel reservations for that night, packed, kissed everyone goodbye, and hopped into the car for what would be a four-hour drive if I timed the traffic right.

Now, I love a good long drive. I have satellite radio, which allows me to listen to whatever I want, be it music, news, sports, for the entire trip.

But I'm also a worrier. I'm the nervous type. And now I'm pretty sure something is "not right" at Southport. I have this strange gut feeling, so I listen to CNBC for the entire four-hour drive, constantly turning over in my head two questions: What does Burns want?

But more importantly, what is going on in this place?

CHAPTER 24

Southport Lane's Office
350 Madison Ave
21st floor

It has been over four months since I first met Alex Burns and the crew at Southport. Each time I walk in the place, the faces are different. But what remains the same is the odd sense of hope tinged with disappointment as you look at the faces of these aspiring deal makers desperately going through the ancient art of dial and smile.

As the only Southport person I respected told me, "This isn't exactly the 'A' team of finance" sitting at the trading desks and in the offices ringing the floor. But to be fair, neither am I.

The difference between me and them is that I know how to run a business. Most of these guys think they can run a business because they can explain the stock price. That's not the way it works.

As I arrive this morning, everyone is on the phone. But apparently no one knows what the person next to them is doing. There's no plan, no strategy, no general investment philosophy that guides them. Everyone is an independent contractor trying to put a deal together that Alex will agree to fund so they can cop a big fat fee and then move on to the next deal.

Over in one corner of the office, always behind closed doors, are the insurance guys. Southport owns four insurance companies: Dallas National Insurance, which they renamed Freestone Insurance; Imperial Insurance; Redwood Insurance; and something called Southport Re (for reinsurance).

The insurance guys preen about the office, projecting a sense of self-importance and superiority. Once, they literally snickered at me as I walked by. They regarded the vineyard I oversaw as a joke.

At Alex's suggestion, I tried to get them to give me a quote for insuring the entire vineyard operation. The Grand Poohbah of the insurance group laughed, said he would get right back to me, and hung up. I never heard from him about the quote.

I did hear from him again, though. He and his crew were staying at the vineyard house having a "strategy retreat" in January 2014. Suddenly, he rediscovered my phone number, called me at my home in Boston, and instructed me to have more firewood sent over "immediately."

Not only that, but one of his guys also told me that the hot water faucet in one of the six bathrooms needed to be reset. He complained that it was off about a quarter-inch to half an inch.

What a bunch of pompous dickheads.

To me, none of the folks at Southport Lane, including the insurance jerks, were impressive. I guess I wasn't very impressive to them either. That makes us even, I suppose.

Oh, I did send over the firewood on the afternoon of their last day at the house. It arrived about an hour before they left.

I can be a dickhead, too. But it's more fun to be a subtle one.

***

I made my way to the main conference room and took my customary seat with my back to the window so I could see people coming. It also kept me from being distracted by the great midtown Manhattan view.

I'd printed out four copies of the QuickBooks file I'd created from nearly a year's worth of statements from First Republic Bank. As is my wont, I had a hardcopy back-up to support, with documentation, the bad news I was about to get into.

Alex burst into the room in his usual fast-paced and semi-flailing walking style and, as was his custom, just started asking questions. No greeting, no short moment of informal chat which is de rigueur at many business meetings. He just launched right in.

"When am I going to have audited financial statements for the vineyard, Richard?"

I had no clue how to answer that one, and I immediately realized that Bernstein's comment on the difficulty of getting a clean opinion would not be helpful right now. So, I pretended I did not hear the question and instead slid a copy of my QuickBooks file across the table to him and said, "I've put the transactions from the Premium Wine Acquisition account into a QuickBooks file. There are some entries here I need help on."

Alex quickly interrupted. With a little alarm to his voice, he asked, "Who gave you those bank statements?"

"Daniel sent them to me over the weekend. He said you approved it," I replied.

"Has McGladrey seen these?" he asked.

"Of course not," I said. "Daniel said these were not to be shown to McGladrey without your approval."

"Good." He nodded and muttered in reaction. He seemed relieved at this news. Maybe he was just relieved we followed his direction.

Looking back down at the spreadsheet, I told him, "I need some clarification on a bunch of these transactions. We're gonna need a paper trail for a lot of these if they're to be included in a Form 10 filing with the SEC."

I flipped the pages of the QuickBooks file until I came across a section I pointed at with my pen. I then slid the printout over to Alex.

"I've listed these as 'Transaction Expenses.' I actually have no idea how to categorize them," I said. "I'm also going to need all the paperwork on each of these transactions so we can give it to the auditors for review."

It seemed like a good opportunity to begin setting the stage for McGladrey's position that a clean audit opinion was in doubt. "There has to be a killer paper trail for audit purposes on all of these transactions. Otherwise, we're going to get into a clean audit opinion discussion with McGladrey."

Alex grabbed my copy of the file and my pen and immediately focused on the total listed as Transaction Fees.

"Holy shit!" he exclaimed. "We paid $3.8 million in transaction fees on this?" Alex went quiet for a few seconds, then began typing furiously into his iPhone.

I then asked specifically about the $3,000,000 to Southport Specialty Finance. "Alex, this does not look good. It will attract a lot of attention from the auditors."

Burns then grabbed my pen and wrote these three letters in the space after "Southport Specialty Finance LLC": "S.I.D."

"What's that mean?" I asked.

"Let's just mark that as 'Shit I Did,'" Alex said confidently.

How do you respond to that? I'll tell you how. You just shut up.

I remember sitting there thinking: *Now what do I do? Do I ask for more detail? Leave it alone? Skip to the next item and try to come back to it?* Unsure, I sat there quietly for a bit longer as Alex looked at my file, typing furiously into his phone.

A few moments later, Andrew Scherr walked in and my stomach knotted.

Andrew had worried me from the first time I met him. I'm convinced that his smile and courtly demeanor mask a cold ruthlessness. His sudden appearance this time definitely caught me off guard.

"Hey, what's going on?" Scherr asks. No greeting, no handshake, no "good to see you," and to make matters worse, he doesn't sit down. He's just standing there, directly across the table from me, staring me down. The usual courtliness and charm are nowhere in sight.

"Someone gave Richard the bank statements to the Premium Wine Acquisition account, and he needs some answers to tell the auditors," Burns chimes in.

Andrew waits for a moment and asks, "Why?" He grabs the copy of the file where Burns wrote "SID," flips a few pages, and says, "This is a waste of time. This isn't the company that's going public!" He then looks to Burns, who is obviously playing catch-up to this sudden switch in focus.

"It's not?" I ask.

"No, nooo," Scherr responds, his tone softening. "Where did you get these anyway?"

"Daniel," I say, referring to the junior in-house counsel who forwarded the bank statements to me.

Fortunately, Daniel is also Andrew's cousin. He's a nice kid. Fresh out of law school. Green as all hell. But a good guy. For the last few months, I made a habit of going through Daniel when I needed something from Southport. Daniel's ability to deliver was pretty good. I tried the senior counsel Darren a few times, but he never so much as returned my phone calls.

Darren always seemed to be in a daze. I asked him a question one time. He looked at me, thought for a moment, then turned and walked in the opposite direction.

It was a simple question, too.

***

From my first exposure to Southport, I realized that dealing with Alex on day-to-day matters was more than a little problematic. Our Jimmy Neutron was clearly the mercurial type. Funny, charming, and pretty bright sometimes. Screaming, insulting, and condescending at others.

I also noticed that pretty much everyone there lived in a kind of fear or paranoia about Alex. It reminded me of an old episode of "The Twilight Zone," the Rod Serling TV show of the 1960s.

In one episode, "It's a Good Life" (Season 3, Episode 8, first broadcast November 3, 1961), we are introduced to the Fremont family of Peaksville, Ohio. A mother and father are living with their son Anthony. But Anthony is no normal child. He's a monster who can transform people into half-man, half-beasts and consign them to the cornfield, never to come inside again. He did it once to his Aunt Amy because she was singing a sad song.

See, Anthony doesn't like singing, and all the people in Peaksville have to smile, think happy thoughts, and say happy things because if they displease Anthony, he can and will wish horrible things on them. Everyone was scared stiff of Anthony. So nothing was more important than making little Anthony happy.

My best Rod Serling imitation careens through my head, "Ladies and Gentlemen, this is Southport Lane."

Early on, I needed to ask Alex a question. Unfamiliar with the basic operating protocols at Southport, I called Jeff to preview the question and get a sense if something was probable. I'll never forget Jeff's answer, "Call him now. He's in a good mood today. Not like yesterday."

Because I was working 75 miles away at the vineyard, I had no way of knowing what variant of Jimmy Neutron was presenting itself on any given day. So I decided I would go through Daniel. He was closer to the mood of the day. Daniel was user-friendly, and he delivered. My kind of guy.

***

Andrew flipped through the pages some more before looking up at me. "Wait, let me apologize for the mix-up here," he said, suddenly switching personas, having now become the polite and courtly Andrew.

"You put all this together? Great work, Richard. Alex and I have been noticing just how much you've accomplished in such a short time."

Uh oh, I thought. *Here it comes.* I wasn't sure what it would be, but the lead-in definitely made my stomach knot a touch more.

"Alex and I are really impressed with the work you've been doing, and noticed the improvements. We would like to bring you in and have you help us with some of our other portfolio companies and investments. We have a lot here that could use your attention. You have a way of getting down to the granular level on these companies in a way most of the folks here do not," he said.

"First, we'd like to make you President and CEO of the company that buys the vineyard," he said. "Southport will still be the majority owner, but you'll be CEO. You have the experience and the background in public markets. Would you be interested in that?"

I personally felt as if we were still so far behind. Outside of cleaning up some of the accounting and beginning to put together a more professional staff, the vineyard was still a financial and operational mess, though less so at the moment because it was the height of the summer season, and being busy hides a lot of underlying problems.

But I was pretty sure they didn't understand that. They knew the revenues had increased substantially. But of course they would—it was August. This was a seasonal business. But I somehow suspected that I was getting credit for the seasonal rise in revenues. If that was true, I'd be a dead man come winter.

"Okay. What does that mean? Another company is going to buy the vineyard, and you want me to head that company?" I asked.

"Exactly!" Andrew responded. "You'll be the President and CEO. You'll get a sizeable amount of stock and higher pay because it's higher risk as a public company. But we know you're the right person for this position."

Burns, quietly staring at his phone, looked up and said, "We can even bring you into some of the other things we're working on. We have a lot of companies in our portfolio that could use your help. It would be a much larger role here at Southport. What do you say?"

Now, in light of the bank statements, the questionable transactions, and the general weirdness I saw all around at Southport, I now had the distinct feeling I was being bought off.

They clearly didn't want auditors or outsiders to see those funky transactions. So they tried to mitigate matters by appealing to my greed, which they assumed was equivalent to theirs. That was a mistake.

The fact is, I'd rather be right than rich. Many people I've dealt with over my long career have seen that as a character flaw. But so be it.

So imagine my surprise when a few seconds later, feeling as if I was having a detached, out-of-body experience, I heard myself answer, "Thank you, I'd be happy to take on greater responsibilities. I look forward to it."

There it was. The old praise and a raise—a time-honored way to get you to accept something you disagree with, and I went along with it.

Satisfied with my answer, Alex and Andrew explained that no one needed to see the QuickBooks spreadsheets I'd prepared.

Shortly thereafter, they both excused themselves. They were busy men, titans of Wall Street even—at least in their minds. Their time and attention were needed elsewhere.

I packed up my things, said a quick hello-goodbye to Jeff, and then headed to my car to drive out to the vineyard.

To this day, I have no idea why Alex had Loren summon me to NYC.

CHAPTER 25

Solar Night Industries Inc

There's a Wall Street the world sees—tall buildings, the Manhattan skyline, the floor of the New York Stock Exchange, CNBC, rich powerful people, etc. Then there's a Wall Street the world doesn't see—smaller firms, undercapitalized companies, less money, shady characters, and a lot—I do mean a lot—of smoke, mirrors, and fakery.

In the Wall Street the world doesn't see, certain people talk a big game. They appear to have all the trappings of movers and shakers. They flash cash and drive luxury cars when they're simply scraping along from deal to deal. Their whole world revolves around the next deal, which, to hear them talk, is always a home run, the ten-bagger, the big one. They're promoters. And guess what promoters do? Promoters promote.

I've seen a lot of this in my career. It has always made me uneasy because rarely do these deals work out the way they're intended. That's because poor planning, poor execution, and poor business fundamentals have a habit of killing a lot of promoters' dreams. Those folks are talkers. They're not doers.

But when the inevitable collapse begins, the promoters are always long gone. They took their "success" fee at the closing and moved on, leaving guys like me to do the clean-up.

This is the world I've inhabited for most of my last 30 years. As a result, I've seen a lot of fraud. I've even resigned from companies that misrepresented the opportunity they were pitching.

I once resigned from a Broker Dealership registered with the Financial Industry Regulatory Authority (FINRA) that wanted me to sign off on a Private Placement Memorandum (PPM). At the time, I had my FINRA Series 24 Principals License. The PPM was chock full of falsehoods and misrepresentations. If I'd signed off on it, I could have been held legally and financially responsible for the abundant untruths contained therein.

Nope. Not me.

But to be fair, without the kinds of guys who make messes wherever they go, there would be no place for guys like me who clean up after them.

For decades, I've dealt with angry and misled investors and creditors. I've been in my share of rooms full of hostile investors and their more unpleasant lawyers.

My pitch to them is usually, "I'm not the cause of the problem, but if we work together, I can be the solution." Sometimes they work with you. Sometimes they just want their pound of flesh. Anybody's flesh. Doesn't matter whose.

But I like being on the right side of things. I don't want to be on the wrong side of regulatory or criminal action when it comes to business dealings. It scares me.

Now, I've been dragged into a couple of regulatory matters. Not as a target but as a witness. Each experience left a horrible taste in my mouth.

In the early 2000s, I was deposed for five hours in New York City by the counsel for a New York State regulator. The subject was a front-page trading scandal involving the big investment bank where I worked. *My involvement?* I was mentioned in an e-mail on an unrelated matter.

My five hours of questioning were preceded by weeks of anxiety. Oh, and let's not forget the $5,000 I had to spend on my attorney—all over an unrelated e-mail whose entire four-word text read, "That's a good thing."

Who needs that?

My father and my grandfather both worked on Wall Street—my grandfather at Goldman Sachs, my father at Smith Barney. Both enjoyed long and fulfilling careers. Both lived the big firm life. Both viewed "the business" as an honorable way to make a living.

My grandfather was a corporate bond trader. My father was a classic money manager. He had clients for decades. He managed money for multiple generations of the same families. He was also a trustee of many trusts, and in more than one case served as a surrogate parent to the trust's beneficiaries.

Every night between late January and April 15, he would sit in our den with stacks of papers on a TV tray. He was doing the taxes for many of his clients—for free.

In retirement, he became a Roman Catholic deacon. He once wrote a sermon entitled, "It's No Sin to Be Rich." It was pretty funny.

But Wall Street today is much more complex and much more hyper-regulated than in my father's and grandfather's day. As my father said for decades after he retired, "I don't recognize the business anymore."

He's right. He wouldn't. Bad stuff that was normal (and permissible) in his day would today get you fined or barred from the industry today. Or prosecuted.

Neither my father nor my grandfather ever got into trouble with the regulators. I didn't want to be the first in the family. As a result, I've always wanted to be the guy people could trust in a shitty situation.

***

A few days after my meeting with Alex and Andrew, I received an e-mail with a hefty attachment from my guy Daniel. It was my introduction to Solar Night Industries, Inc (*Ticker: SLND*).

Southport wanted SLND to own all the stock of Lieb Cellars, Lieb Vineyards, and Premium Wine Group. And as promised during our "Shit I Did" meeting, I was going to be the President and Chief Executive Officer of the new owner.

So, I was now the buyer of all the vineyard entities. In short, I was getting paid by Southport to buy a company owned by Southport, and when the transaction was finished, I'd be getting paid by Southport to be CEO of a company they owned all over again.

But I was already president of all the vineyard entities. Now they wanted me to sell the vineyard companies to a separate company of which I was also president.

Legally, I couldn't be president of both the buying and selling companies. Southport already owned 92 percent of the vineyard companies. Once they were sold to Solar Night Industries, Southport would still own 92 percent of that company. But they still needed to appoint a president of the old companies. Which they did. And Alexander Chatfield Burns appointed none other than... Alexander Chatfield Burns.

While this seemed like a corporate shell game, there was nothing illegal about it. Companies do these types of transactions all the time. If done properly, they can be perfectly legal.

Southport's rationale for the transaction went something like this: Because Solar Night was publicly traded, and if it owned all the assets of the vineyard entities, Solar Night's market capitalization would be much higher than the $12.75 million they paid for the assets of the vineyard entities.

On one occasion, Alex asked me if we could get the value of the vineyard entities to $50 million.

What Southport was trying to do was pull off something called the public-private arbitrage, which works this way: Let's say a private equity firm buys a company for X amount. After several years of ownership, they take the company public for Y amount. If everything works out, the increase in value from X to Y can be more than 10 to 20 fold. Or more. They then claim the increase in value as profit.

But there was only one problem with Southport's approach, and it was a big one.

You see, I've done a lot of public and private valuations in my life. I even took courses in how to do it during the late 1980s-early 1990s at the New York Institute of Finance.

It's a challenging intellectual exercise. I like it. It's like opening a new crime or mystery novel. By the time I finished the valuation, I sometimes knew the company's numbers better than the owners.

Now, I valued the vineyard as a private company at about $5.5 million. As a public company, I concluded that with a little luck, the vineyard might get a valuation of maybe $9.0 million. But they had paid $12.75 million. No matter how many times I did the calculations, I still couldn't get the valuation to exceed the price they paid.

Alex was dead-set on pursuing this nonsensical path. To his credit, I always suspected that Andrew—with an MBA from Yale and a law degree from the University of Baltimore Law School—knew this was a fool's errand.

I opened up the document Daniel had e-mailed me and the 70-page corporate history of Solar Night that came as an attachment. The company began life as "Bernard Haldane Associates" in 2004. In 2005, it changed its name to "Triton Technologies." In 2007, it finally settled in with "Solar Night Industries."

But Alex had other ideas. He was calling me quite often around that time. In one of those calls, he informed me that he wanted-ed Daniel and I to change the name of Solar Night to Premium Beverage Group as soon as possible. Alex added one more thing: He wanted the ticker symbol for Premium Beverage Group to be "PBEV."

Getting the name changed to Premium Beverage Group was a simple exercise. Daniel prepared all the proper forms and corporate resolutions required to change the name. All I did was review and advise. We filed everything with the Nevada state regulators where SLND was domiciled and *voila!* we were Premium Beverage Group Inc.

But getting the ticker symbol changed would be a bit trickier. That required petitioning the Financial Industry Regulatory Authority (FINRA). FINRA is a self-regulating organization. Its job is to police public markets, member brokerage firms, and all the stockbrokers and traders who work for those member firms. In other words, as a regulator, it was the first line of law enforcement. As a result, they could make your life miserable. They could scrap your best laid plans, and they could sanction and fine you out of existence.

I had no idea how much scrutiny FINRA would give Solar Night as we prepared to present them our latest corporate acrobatics.

I Googled the people involved in selling Solar Night Industries to Southport. I was looking for what regulators call "bad actors." These are people who've been in regulatory trouble, and I try to avoid them at all costs because regulators have long memories and will undoubtedly focus on your bad actor.

In the Wall Street you see, big law firms who charge a thousand dollars an hour frequently sign off on a transaction with an "Opinion of Counsel" affidavit. This is a document which speaks to the truth, accuracy, and lawfulness of the representations and warranties made by their client. These big firms have reputations to maintain. They have malpractice insurance in case they make an error. In short, they have money to back up their claims.

In the Wall Street you don't see, you are always on the lookout for bad actors. An "Opinion of Counsel" from a small-time solo practitioner always triggers a little extra scrutiny by regulators.

So imagine my surprise when I learned that the law license of one of the sellers' attorneys had been suspended. He had also been disbarred in another state. When I brought this to Alex Burns' attention, he said, "No big deal. We're not going to use that guy."

Welcome to the Wall Street you don't see.

CHAPTER 26

A few days later, I received a call from Alex's assistant Loren. She told me I'd be receiving a FedEx package at my home that afternoon. She didn't know what was in it, just some documents for me to sign. But she did make it very clear to me that I needed to sign them and return them to Alex that very afternoon. A return envelope and completed air bill were in the package as well.

Well, that got my attention.

My curiosity piqued, I gave Jeff a call to see if he knew what was coming. He did. The package contained the corporate resolutions appointing me President and Chief Executive Officer. I was also being appointed as the second member of the two-person board of directors of Solar Night Industries.

Seems Southport only thought it necessary to have two board members— Jeff and me. Now, boards of directors can have as many or as few members as the shareholders want. Usually, the number of required board members is set forth in the corporate by-laws. Two seemed too few. But hey, it was their show.

It was also a Friday, in summer's waning days. Because I lived on the south shore of Boston, I was kind of itching to get down to the harbor so my wife and I could hit my favorite restaurant.

Our beachy little tourist town had hundreds of pleasure boats—sail and power—moored in the harbor. If you didn't get seated at this restaurant by 5:00 pm, you wouldn't get in until 8:00 or 9:00 pm.

To quote an old friend, "I don't wait to get into Le Cirque."

I completely agree with that sentiment. We love this harbor restaurant, but it ain't no Le Cirque. No way I'm hanging around to get in there that late.

The FedEx package finally arrived. I grabbed it and quickly closed myself off in my makeshift home office.

I opened the package and found three documents as well as the return envelope and air bill. Jeff was right. There was a corporate resolution appointing me to the following positions:

- President
- Treasurer
- Secretary
- Member of the board of directors.

Jeff was also listed as a member of the board as well. He also signed the resolution as the "Sole Director and Officer."

There was also another resolution signed by Jeff. This one authorized Solar Night to issue up to 50,000 shares of preferred stock. I'd read the 70-page informational package a few days earlier. There were no preferred shares, either issued or outstanding.

Okay, I thought. They're giving themselves the flexibility to issue stock in the future. That made sense.

Next, I pulled out a piece of paper I'd come to regret ever seeing. It was a Preferred Stock Certificate. It looked like it was printed on someone's desktop computer, even down to being printed on ordinary white copy paper.

It was filled out. It only needed the signatures of the Secretary of the corporation, which I'd learned a few seconds ago... *was me!*

It carried certificate number 464. As if there were already 463 certificates of Preferred Stock issued. It constituted 20,000 of the 50,000 shares authorized just the day before. According to the "certificate," the shares were issued to "Southport Specialty Finance."

Making matters worse, Southport Specialty Finance was also "selling and transferring" those very same 20,000 shares immediately to Redwood Reinsurance. Redwood was a Southport-owned reinsurance company based in the Cayman Islands. I knew nothing about it. Had never even heard of it before.

And wasn't Southport Specialty Finance the recipient of the $3,000,000 that made Alex Burns' list of "Shit I Did"? So, they get three million dollars from Premium Wine Acquisition, and now they're getting 20,000 preferred shares of the company that doesn't even own the vineyard yet? This was screwy.

Also of note, the transfer section to Redwood was signed by none other than Alexander Chatfield Burns.

I stared at the certificate for a few minutes. My mind was racing. There was so much I didn't know, and that made me nervous. Out of habit, I started making a list of questions. I was holding the pen so tightly that, after a few minutes, my hand got a cramp.

I put down the pen and called Jeff again. I needed answers. But he was unsure about the money trail as well. We both agreed this was an unusual way to conduct business. He suggested I call Alex. Which I did. Immediately.

Alex had skipped out of Manhattan early to beat the traffic to the east end of Long Island. He was spending the weekend with a group at the vineyard estate house, which he now called "my house." The master bedroom was now "my room." No one was allowed in it.

One of my less than pleasant tasks that summer was cleaning up after Alex and his "friends" had visited his house. Whoever they were, they were slobs. Most Monday nights or Tuesday mornings when I arrived, the house looked like it'd been the scene of a college rager the night before. Half-empty wine glasses were everywhere. Plates with the last meal's remainders were still sitting on the tables. It was as if the dinner had ended only moments before. A cake—now stale and hardened—with a knife still in it was sitting on the hardwood island in the chef's kitchen. The bathrooms sometimes looked and smelled like they'd been used on concert night at Madison Square Garden.

Cigar butts—lots of them—were in glasses and flowerpots. Many were stomped out on the patio, or my personal favorite, floating in the pool. I don't need to go into detail what that looked like.

I was told at one point that one of his guests asked if they should clean up before leaving. Alex apparently replied, "We have people who do that" and walked out.

Yeah. Me, at least initially.

But thank God for the cleaning service that came in behind me. They earned every cent we paid them.

From the very beginning to the very end of my time with the

company, that house was a source of endless irritation to me. People loved that house. Not me. Something was always broken and the fix was never cheap.

Alex and others at Southport regularly let their friends and friends of friends and colleagues use it for a weekend. Many took home various souvenirs. I finally had to put a double-lock on the wine cellar door. Some people took that as an affront and called to complain. Most never even said thank you.

During that first summer, I actually slept on the huge couch in the home movie theater in the basement. The house was surrounded by 25-plus acres of vineyard. During the day, it was beautiful. But at night, if you were alone, it was kind of creepy.

But every week, I packed up whatever garbage I'd created and brought it home to Massachusetts. I'd also unload the two massive dishwashers which the cleaning service left chock full of Alex's exploits the previous weekend.

I only allowed myself to use one of the six bathrooms—the one in the basement near the movie theater. So I cleaned it and got out of there. I didn't want to leave any sign of having been there during the week.

***

So, after hanging up with Jeff, I called Alex. If I were a betting man, I'd say he was already well past his first bottle of wine.

First thing out of his mouth was that he was glad I called. He wanted to know where the big red Kitchen Aid mixer was. He wanted to do some baking.

I told him where it was. I wish I'd said, "It's right where you found it last time when you baked that stale-ass cake I found a few weeks ago." But of course, I didn't.

Having learned where the mixer was, he was ready to hang up when I asked him about the Preferred Stock.

"What about it?" he replied.

Whenever I'm a bit nervous, I talk really fast.

"What's it for? Why is Southport Specialty Finance selling it to Redwood? What was the purchase price consideration? Where's the subscription agreement? Has the State of Nevada been informed?

Where's the documentation for this?"

Finally, I blurted out the most important question, "How much is it for?"

I have to admit, this kid was smooth. Without missing a beat, he dumped it all back to me, which caught me completely off-guard.

"Richard, after I reviewed your spreadsheet, we knew we needed to clean this up a bit. This is how we intend to do that. You need to do a few things to help. First, go through your spreadsheet and separate out all the vineyard-related stuff from the non-vineyard related stuff. The vineyard related stuff will be the amount of the preferred. Second, get the lawyers working on the documentation for the preferred shares away. We can clean all this up next week."

And Redwood?" I asked.

"That is where the money came from," he replied.

At first blush, it all seemed plausible. It made sense. It was totally backwards process-wise. But if it all got done, then we had a proper paper trail. Good. I could fix this.

So, I signed the Preferred Stock Certificate. I put it into the return envelope. On the way to our favorite harbor front restaurant, we put it into a FedEx drop box with moments to spare before pickup. But it was still nagging at me.

A short time later, and after a proper martini or two, I realized I'd regret signing that certificate.

***

The Wall Street you don't see frequently impales itself upon its inability to do the little things right.

Process matters. Paperwork matters. Full disclosure matters. Doing things in the proper sequence matters. Proper reviews by competent attorneys and accountants matter.

It just didn't matter to Alex and Andrew. These guys talked a great game, but their inattention to detail and process was obvious from the start.

During this time, Alex and I began speaking often. He began asking me if I'd look at some of their other companies—but not the insurance companies. They were sacrosanct.

Unsurprisingly, nearly every one of the possible private equity investments I looked at were dogs. After dealing with the vineyard for nearly four months, I was pretty sure why. It was simple.

They had no idea what they were doing.

They were overpaying for crummy companies. But this many purchases of crummy companies smelled like job security to me. I saw a lifetime of fat paychecks cleaning up after these stupid fucks.

It was also around this time, perhaps feeling a bit full of myself, that I lectured Alex a bit. "Alex, private equity is a process-driven endeavor, and you ignore that process at your peril."

His dismissive, sarcastic, and pissy response: "I know how to do deals, Richard."

No, he didn't. He didn't have a fucking clue.

CHAPTER 27

September 18, 2013

Until today, all I knew was that Southport Lane was a quirky private equity firm that had no clue how to do private equity investing.

By the end of the day, it seemed highly likely that Southport was involved in a scam or a crime and I had to figure out exactly how.

I simply could not understand how people this incompetent—and this bizarre—could be managing this much money. Not legitimately at least.

I've been around Wall Street firms all my life. My grandfather was the President of the National Securities Traders Association (NSTA) as well as the Securities Traders of New York (STANY). He was also a senior guy at Goldman Sachs. We grew up with tales of my grandfather renting a train and going around the country picking up all the traders going to the National Convention in San Diego.

A lover of dry martinis, he would buy a case of gin before each trip. Before he left, he would take out one bottle of gin that he'd packed and replace it with a bottle of vermouth. He would always come home with half a bottle of vermouth and no gin, my grandmother joked.

One of my favorite things to do as a kid in the 1960s was to go into my father's office at White Weld & Company in New Haven and write down all the ticker symbols and the numbers next to them as they scrolled across the big loud ticker-tape machine stretching across an entire office wall.

These visits were nearly always followed by a visit to my favorite Italian restaurant, Marra's. Unsurprisingly, my dad knew everyone in the joint, and everybody knew him. Me? They all knew me too. I was treated like a prince.

All this was long before computers, and even before Quotron stock price monitors, were on every broker's desks. Senior White Weld guys would come over to my father's desk and ask me for the last trade of their favorite stocks. I was their Quotron! I loved it!

Reared in an era of a Wall Street long gone, I'm nonetheless unable to shake my image of Wall Street money managers as serious, sober, cautious, experienced, and... restrained people.

By the end of the day, it was indelibly clear to me that Southport Lane's management was none of these things.

Alex and Andrew were so secretive, even evasive on the origins of the firm. My buddy Jeff, who was President of Southport, could not explain how they got control of these insurance companies. I was already suspicious of Alex—or at least aware that he could bullshit with the best of them. It was clear to me he didn't go to Yale or own and race a 60-foot Swan sailboat. But he persisted in telling these lies.

One other thing was certain: I liked the paycheck, and I really liked running the vineyard. I enjoyed being back on my feet after a year on the business sidelines. I was determined to keep the vineyard alive... and to continue getting paid.

***

Around 2002, Jeff had introduced me to Brad Hoecker. Brad, who became a friend, is a traditional private equity guy. He's also very smart. Someone once told me he was one of the top graduates in his class at Northwestern Business School. After Northwestern, he got a job with the private equity arm of Merrill Lynch, the financial giant. At some point in the early 1990s, Merrill spun off the private equity arm to its managers.

After the spin-off, they renamed their firm Stonington Partners. They managed something like $2 billion. By the time I met him, Brad had worked his way up to partner. Their office, on the 48th floor of the General Motors Building, was simply gorgeous. It was precisely what comes to mind when you think of a $2 billion investment fund.

Anyway, Brad was impressive. He also made me nervous.

See, I can be a little obsessive-compulsive. If I have an idea about something, especially something I think is important, I hyper-focus on it. I'll block everything out and turn the idea over and over in my head. I can do that for hours. It's my favorite pastime while driving. I've driven from home to mid-town Manhattan, a four-to-five-hour drive, with no radio, no music. Nothing. All I have is the idea I'm trying to pick apart and analyze. To me, it's fun.

When I think I have my issue all figured out, I take my hypotheses for a test drive, usually by calling and running them by a friend with some expertise in that area. All my friends and family know that when I call them out of the blue and start the call with, "Got a minute?" they're in for a much longer conversation.

It's probably why so many of my calls go into voicemail and never get returned.

So, what made me so nervous talking to Brad in those early days? Simple. After all those obsessive-compulsive thoughts spinning in my head, Brad always asked me a question or two I wasn't prepared for. He still does it now.

Brad's old firm had dissolved a few years before. Too many new private equity firms started during the 1990s and early 2000s. They were all chasing the same institutional investors. Stonington Partners became a casualty as a result.

In September 2013, Brad and a group had an opportunity and were looking for a financial partner. We talked about it several times. He showed me his financial models. Everything made sense.

I liked it. A lot. It was simple. It solved a big problem for a globally recognized consumer products company.

I'd been in that position before.

In 1998, I led the investment in a small company that simplified a supply chain problem for a global semiconductor company. That small company went from $3 million in revenues to $30 million in revenues in 14 months.

It also taught me valuable lessons. If a small company can solve a problem for a global behemoth, you know three things right away:

- First, the little company makes a quality product.
- Second, they deliver it on time.
- Third, they do both at a competitive price.

No one understands a vertical market better than the purchasing agent of a global company. Getting a purchasing agent at a global company to pay attention to you isn't easy. They're not going to risk their resources or their reputations on you if you can't deliver. Before they will give you even a dollar of business, they will put you through your paces. It's called the Vendor Approval Process. But once you are an approved vendor, they can give you all the business you can handle. And more.

Their endorsement, even in the form of a simple purchase order, carries enormous credibility for an investor-operator like me.

Brad and his group had a solution to a problem for one of the most famous brands in the world. They had the technology and capability to take millions of gallons of excess or contaminated soft drink syrup and turn it into ethanol.

Even better, the major global company would pay them to take the waste off their hands. That means not only did they have no raw materials cost, but their raw material supplier would pay them! Their only costs would be their manufacturing costs. Who doesn't love that?

The biggest risk was the price of ethanol. But ethanol is a global commodity bought and sold on the Chicago Board of Trade. There's even a futures market which will allow you to lock in your sale price weeks, even months, in advance. As long as the ethanol market didn't crash, they could pretty much guarantee their profit.

I loved this deal. So did Jeff. Together, we convinced both Brad and Alex Burns that it might be a good idea to sit down and discuss Southport as the new company's chief financial sponsor.

I really wanted Southport to make this investment. It was important to me. I trusted Brad.

It was also a chance for Southport to make a quality investment. Unlike the balance of their portfolio, which was a complete mess.

Did I also want to show the Southport guys, especially Alex, the proper way to get a deal done? You bet I did.

The meeting was set for 1:00 pm. I'd driven in from the vineyard earlier and used the little conference room next to Alex's office.

Occasionally, Alex would pop his head into where I was sitting to ask me questions or shoot the shit. At about 11:45 am, he asked me to go to lunch with him. We walked about three or four blocks to some place he liked. Alex speed- walks. Even in mid-town Manhattan at lunch time. Now, I'm a big guy; I had trouble keeping up.

As we ate our sandwiches, he asked me if I wanted to work at Southport full time. I told him that he hired me to fix the vineyard, and that was a long way from being stable. But I did say that if he liked the deal with Brad, I'd like to run that deal for Southport.

Besides, it would take a team of people to fix Southport's God-awful portfolio. The idea was interesting to me. The portfolio certainly was dog shit. But the people and the politics at Southport… well, let's just say a lot of people would have to admit mistakes. That would be bloody. I just didn't see that happening.

On the walk back to the office, we very briefly discussed the upcoming meeting with Brad. I emphasized again that these were the types of people he wanted to be affiliated with. Left unsaid was the rag-tag nature of most of the Southport crew.

At 1:00 pm, Brad arrived. Jeff and I met him in the office lobby and brought him into the conference room, where the three of us waited for Alex.

A few minutes later, Alex arrived with Rob McGraw in tow. I knew who Rob was but hadn't interacted with him in the previous months. He was a quiet guy. On the young side, maybe mid to late 30s. Seemed pleasant enough. I didn't know what he did at Southport. But by bringing him into this meeting, I took that as a sign that this was someone Alex trusted.

Brief introductions made, I outlined how I knew Brad and his background. I also spoke of the work that I did with him on a semiconductor deal a few years earlier during the waning days of Stonington Partners. We were trying to buy a division of NXP, the semiconductor giant. It was owned by KKR and Bain Capital at the time. All that was true, but in reality, I was just name-dropping to help set the stage.

Alex was quiet. As usual, he was staring down at this phone. But during Brad's presentation, Rob McGraw asked a few very good questions. Rob, it was clear, was a very bright guy. His questions were clear and articulate, and showed a deep understanding of financial structure. I was impressed. What was he doing at Southport?

At one point during the meeting, I did grow a bit concerned. Alex could become defensive at times. When Brad answered a question, he was smart, well-reasoned, and knew his material. For some reason, this caught Alex off guard.

Alex wasn't reacting to Brad in a blatantly pissy way. But it did seem that he needed to prove he was smart too. Anyway, it didn't last long.

About a half-hour later, Brad finished his presentation. Rob asked a few more questions. He was definitely a smart guy. Jeff was pretty quiet.

Alex then looked to me and said, "What do you think, Richard?"

My answer was unequivocal. "I like it," I said, "They have the buy side lined up. They have the sell side lined up. Hell, they can even hedge out their sell-side pricing. They have the facility. They just need money for equipment to make the magic happen. Maybe some working capital support. We get a fee on the through-put and an equity kicker. I know these guys. I've worked with them in the past. They're smart, they're honest, and this will make us money. We should do this."

Alex was again staring down on his phone. It was clear he was thinking.

After maybe twenty seconds, he looked up and said, "Okay, I'll do it. Richard, you run the deal."

No transaction screening memo. No site visits. No financial models. No investment committee memos. No committee meetings. That is all it took. Alex Burns, the frequently self-described smartest guy in the room, had committed $15 million to an investment he'd learned about only minutes before.

Never one to hang around and chit chat, Alex got up from his chair and began heading to the door when Brad said, "Hey Alex, before you go?"

I winced. Brad wasn't done yet.

"Alex, how did you come to control all these insurance companies?" Brad asked.

There it was. A total Brad Hoecker moment. See, Brad has a way of asking the most difficult, the most cringe-worthy questions, but not in a threatening way. He's polite. But he's firm and business-like.

No emotion. No conveyance of skepticism. No embarrassment felt or conveyed. He just lays it out there.

Alex stopped in the doorway, pivoted on his heel, turned toward Brad with a smirk, thought for a moment, and then said: "Jesus with a telescope on Mars couldn't figure out how I did it."

He then pivoted back toward the door and walked out.

I was dumbfounded. Jeff sat there looking perplexed as well. Brad looked over at the two of us, his mouth slightly agape, his eyes wide open.

Suddenly, it was like we all had had the same thought at the same time. The three of us began stuffing papers into our backpacks and suit coat pockets. Without saying a word, we got up and headed toward the elevators in the lobby.

Waiting for the elevator, one of us started to snicker. As the elevator door opened, we all hopped in, still stifling the urge to laugh.

"Not yet… not yet," I murmured. "Wait until we're outside."

We were all trying not to guffaw in unison as we went down 22 floors to the lobby. When the elevator doors opened, we all sped to the revolving door. We must have looked like three guys who desperately needed a bathroom. Any bathroom.

When we hit the sidewalk of Madison Ave, we turned left and walked 15 feet before we all erupted in a huge laugh fit. People walking by probably thought we were either nuts or some overdressed street performers.

"Oh my God!" Jeff exclaimed.

"What the fuck did he just say?" I said, my chest heaving in laughter.

"He did not say that, did he?" Brad asked. "That was ridiculous."

"Why would he say that?" Jeff said.

In our business, it was without question one of the most inane and outrageous things to say to someone. What made it worse was that he was dead serious. He meant it.

Jeff and I started to calm down. But we were still slightly in shock.

Brad then turned to us and in a calm and sober tone said, "Guys, you need to be careful. Something is very, very wrong here. I'm serious. Something is seriously wrong."

He was right, of course.

Jeff mentioned something about updating his resumé.

Up until that moment, Southport had been just a quirky private equity firm that wasn't very good at private equity. But after that statement, I couldn't see it that way anymore.

Brad was right. Something was deeply, deeply wrong.

But I was sure of one other thing. I wasn't going anywhere. I was hooked.

CHAPTER 28

December 2013
Three Months Later

As the year drew to a close, I remained certain that something was seriously amiss at Southport Lane. Yet nothing in particular stood out.

Well, actually, lots of things stood out. But after a while, you become desensitized to day-to-day ridiculousness.

In distressed situations, it's almost never one thing that brings the place down. It's usually a confluence of factors.

But after the "Jesus with a telescope on Mars" lunacy, I became much more cautious, and I became much more formal in my dealings with the folks at Southport.

Elliot Spitzer had a famous line when he was New York Attorney General: "Never write when you can speak, never speak when you can nod, and never, ever use e-mail."

I had that line seared into my psyche after being deposed for five hours over a four-word e-mail—"that's a good thing"—in 2002.

But with Southport, I went in the opposite direction. I began to communicate almost exclusively by e-mail. I wanted a written record.

Why? As a wise lawyer (my brother, Tom) told me years ago, "The paper trail is the case in litigation." And I was now certain that at some point, there would be litigation.

As summer drifted into fall and fall slipped into winter, Alex became increasingly erratic. There were still a lot of problems at the vineyard, and when it came to major decisions—the vineyard was Alex's baby, don't forget—I needed to run them by Alex.

For example, Alex had commissioned Peter, the branding consultant, to redecorate the vineyard house. By July, the cost had ballooned to $93,343, and some of the vendors were getting itchy to get paid.

What's worse, Peter had personally contracted with these vendors. That meant the vendor checks covering these costs had to be made out to Peter. Before I arrived, Peter went directly to Alex, and Alex authorized payment.

Not anymore.

Now Peter had to submit those invoices to me. I then had to go to Southport to get them paid. Southport was now asking for more documentation, and properly so. That was fine with me. It made sense. But as much as I liked Peter, he and documentation were not close friends. So, I had a lot of tap dancing to do to get those bills paid.

Though high on my priority list, the preferred stock issued in August was still only some ink on a piece of copy paper. No documents. No state filings. Nothin'. Yet it was the only document representing $1.2 million spent by Southport for the benefit of the vineyard. That was $1.2 million over and above the $12.75 million Southport had paid for the vineyard less than six months earlier.

Now, my normal line of problem resolution was to contact Daniel first. But he kicked the problem up to Darren, the general counsel. I found it difficult to get Darren's attention. But when I did on this issue, he kicked it up to Alex.

Finally, when I got the issue to Alex in late September, he told me he was rethinking the entire preferred stock issue. He had an idea on how he could get the preferred stock to trade on an exchange.

He and I had a subsequent phone discussion on how to make that work. It ended with no resolution.

Now remember, I'm still trying to get the vineyard's financial statements audited. The preferred stock issue would never fly with the auditors. But Alex didn't seem to care.

Alex was also sending late-night, flame-throwing e-mails to the auditors. He accused them of everything from sheer incompetence to padding the bills. The next morning, the auditor's first call was always to me. That was fun. After a while, I just agreed with the auditors. They were right and Alex was unreasonable.

My hands were tied on so many issues at the vineyard.

For example, we had almost six years of finished product inventory on hand—around 20,000 cases of wine in the warehouse. Because it was fall and harvest was in full swing, it would increase to seven years' worth in a month or two.

I got my start in the steel manufacturing business. As a result, I always viewed excess inventory as dead money. I didn't care that it was wine and the wine romantics thought it appreciated in value over time.

Every time I walked into that warehouse, I saw dead dollar signs. I also saw one less time that I'd have to ask Southport for money to cover payroll. I even explored selling the surplus wine to foreign exporters for cheap.

But no. Alex said that we would need all that inventory for when we would be selling 50,000 cases per year. Yeah, right. We were selling 3,700 cases a year at the time. 50,000 cases per year? That was a grand fucking delusion.

I should add here that Alex's girlfriend's best friend was still on the payroll during this time. She was listed as a salesperson. Now, she was a lovely kid. But she was getting $3,000 a month for a no-show job. She probably sold a little bit of wine here or there. But still...

Finally, three phone calls stick out as evidence that Alex and Southport were becoming more and more unstable.

My wife and I were in Holliston, MA at our sons' Friday night football game in November. It was the state playoffs. Holliston was undefeated, and my son's team was ahead at the half. It was about 8:30 pm and the third quarter had just started when my phone rang. It was Alex. I was pretty immersed in the gridiron goings-on, so I let it go to voice mail.

Then he called again. I let it go into voice mail. This time he left a message. It was vile. It was unhinged.

A moment later, he called a third time. Like an idiot, I answered.

Alex ripped into me in a way I don't think anyone in my life ever has. My immediate impression was that he was drunk or high. He was certainly spitting mad. And when I say spitting, you could actually hear him spitting into the phone.

I walked away from my wife and headed towards the end zone

where no one could hear. I decided to keep my mouth shut and let him spew.

The Super Bowl was being held at the Meadowlands in a few months, and somehow Alex had heard that I'd signed up Lieb Cellars to sponsor an event in New York City in the run-up to the game on Sunday. He was right. I had.

My good friend, Kristen Kuliga, is a football players' agent and sports marketing guru. She has her fingers in more pro sports-related things than you could count.

When our son tore his ACL in the last game of his sophomore season, she got us in with the New England Patriots Medical Group. Reid had his knee operated on at the facility next to Gillette Stadium. The waiting room looked directly onto the playing field.

Kristen had arranged for Lieb to be a sponsor of a week-long wine and beer tasting event. It would be located right next to Madison Square Garden. We would be the wine sponsor. Our wines, and only our wines, would be served.

It was a great deal for us. The sponsorship was free, and would garner us a huge amount of free publicity. Even better, we got to sell our wine to the event, albeit at a deeply discounted price.

Whoever told Alex about our role in the event failed to tell him the terms. He screamed that I was paying $10,000 for sponsorship and giving the wine away for free.

The exact opposite was true.

After letting him go off for what felt like most of the third quarter, I finally told him the actual terms of the sponsorship. When I was done, the phone went silent for a few seconds. He then said, "Oh! Good job!" and hung up.

A week later, he called on another matter. It was as if the previous Friday screamfest had never occurred. He was perfectly pleasant. Then he told me in no uncertain terms, "I'm appointing you to the board of Massive Interactive. You'll represent Southport."

I'd heard of them through Jeff. It was his deal. So this was extremely awkward. Jeff was one of my closest friends.

Now, I didn't have the faintest idea what Massive Interactive did. I knew that they were in London and they were some kind of tech company. I didn't even get a chance to ask about them before he hung up. A few minutes later, the corporate resolution came via e-mail appointing me to the board.

Less than a week earlier, he was calling me a fucking idiot. Now he was appointing me to the board of another company.

This was getting kooky.

***

In early December, I received a call from Rob McGraw. I liked Rob. He was very smart. In the few interactions I'd had with him, he came across as a rational voice in an increasingly irrational place.

But I wasn't prepared for this.

"Hey, what's your plan to repay the vineyards debt?" he asked.

Confused, I answered, "Debt? What debt? There's the preferred stock, technically, but there's no debt. We're at the tail end of an audit... There's no debt here!"

That's when he told me, "The vineyard has $25 million in debt. We need a plan for how you're going to pay it back."

"Rob!" I continued, "There's no debt on our books. Southport owns this place free and clear! We've had auditors and an audit prep firm here for over six months. There's no debt. This has to be a mistake."

He was insistent. I was dumbfounded.

The conversation ended pretty much there. He insisted the vineyard owed $25 million. I was sure it didn't. He didn't offer details. He wouldn't even tell me who we owed the money to.

This had to be a mix-up. Weird stuff regularly happened at Southport which no one could or would explain.

***

The year 2013 ended with Alex and me alone at the vineyard's estate house. Alex had been there for a few days between Christmas and New Year's.

He had chartered a private jet to fly his girlfriend and her mother and their dog to Long Island for a few days. I got there at about 1:00 pm on December 30th. The girlfriend, mother, and dog had left earlier in the day—back on the private jet, I presumed.

When I showed up, I was happy the house wasn't a pigsty. I chalked that up to Alex having his girlfriend and mother visiting.

Alex had told me he was leaving the next morning to head back to the city. Good. I had a fair amount on my agenda and many issues were coming to a head. All required Alex's sign-off.

Even more important, Alex had given me permission to have my wife and two sons stay at the house for New Year's Eve, as long as nobody went into "his room."

Once Alex was gone, my wife and two sons (ages 15 and 18) showed up. Our son, Reid, was still on crutches awaiting surgery in early January. The vineyard house had huge couches (Reid is 6'7") so he would be very comfortable. Besides, he needed a change of scenery. He'd been stuck inside our house since his injury in November. Alex, our oldest, had finished his first semester of college.

Once they arrived, I was looking forward to a fun New Year's Eve—good food, good wine, and cut-throat card games.

But before the fun could begin, there was business to attend to. I had a long list of open items I needed to run by Alex, who was in an extremely gregarious mood. He was also chain-smoking cigars from his wine-cellar humidor.

First, we executed the merger documents between the vineyard entities and Premium Beverage Group Inc, (PBEV). Alex signed as the seller. I as President of PBEV signed as the buyer. The vineyards were now a public company, and I was its Chairman, President, and Chief Executive Officer.

Alex found that a worthy reason for opening a good bottle of wine. I suspect it was not his first of the day. He offered me a cigar. I passed. Cigars and I have a long and antagonistic history.

Next, I needed to nail down the documentation from the preferred stock we had issued in August. To my surprise and great relief, he told me he was going to cancel it and issue common stock instead.

Fine with me. Cleaner too. Cross that off the list.

Finally, I told him about my call from Rob McGraw a few weeks earlier. So, I asked Alex straight out.

"Does the vineyard have $25 million in debt to repay? We're a public company now. That changes everything," I said.

Alex's response was memorable.

"Richard, whoever told you that there's $25 million in debt here doesn't know what they're talking about! There's no debt."

Oh boy.

CHAPTER 29

January 2014

A new year, but same shit show. Only now I'm in deeper.

I thought I'd sidestepped the question of working full-time for Southport a few months earlier. But on January 4th, I started as a Managing Director of Southport Lane. I went from being a consultant to being an employee. But at the same time, I was still President and CEO of the public company that owned the vineyard. So that was my first priority.

Alex celebrated my elevation by sending an iPad to my house. I gave it to my son Reid to keep him occupied while recovering from knee surgery.

A few months earlier, Darren the General Counsel left—more like disappeared. It took me a few weeks to realize he was gone. No wonder he wasn't returning my phone calls.

Frankly, I found Darren vague and not very helpful anyway... when I could get a hold of him. So, I can't say I was sad to see him go.

Darren's replacement, Hugh, seemed like a decent enough guy. Smart, responsive, big firm background. That could only be a positive, right? They also hired Bob Yingling, who I'd been introduced to a few years earlier on a different deal to come in as CFO. I didn't know Bob well. But people respected him. Maybe there was reason for hope.

But all the personnel changes in the world didn't change the fact that something was "very, very wrong." Brad Hoeker's assessment and admonishment remained stuck in my head.

After all, Alex Burns was... well... Alex Burns. He wasn't remotely as smart as he thought he was, and it was clear he had no fidelity to the truth. Could Hill and Yingling put guard rails around him? That was my hope. But this was not a stable organization.

To make matters worse, money suddenly seemed to be tight. It wasn't sloshing around like it had been during the summer. I had a lot of suspicions about what was wrong, but no proof.

A grad school professor of mine (and one I quite admired) frequently said to me, "Learning is the tension between question and answer."

When it came to Southport at the beginning of 2014, well, there was only tension. Plenty of questions but no answers.

At the vineyard, I was also going through my first January. As I'd see over and over throughout the next few years, revenue in January drops off the cliff. But payroll doesn't. So, money gets tight fast. There was no way we were getting through the month, let alone the winter, without cash assistance from Southport.

On top of that, Alex decided back in the late fall that he wanted Lieb to make a hard sparkling cider. Why? Because he liked hard, sparkling cider. He had brought it up several times in the previous months, so I knew he was serious.

I'd made Ami Opisso Lieb's general manager on January 1st. Smart, organized, and focused, she was a natural for the job. Other employees naturally gravitated to her if they had problems and questions. I watched her solve those problems smoothly and effortlessly. It had been an easy choice.

So, I asked her to figure out the cost and steps to bring a hard sparkling cider to market. She was the only one with the smarts and experience to plan out how to bring a new product to market. I had no idea. She did a fantastic job.

But to do all this, I also needed to sit down with Alex. I had to make sure he understood how much money it would take to bring the new product to market *and* survive the winter.

Things were also sounding dicey at Southport. Jeff told me that one of their insurance partners was on the warpath. They wanted their money back on some investments Southport sold them. As a result, Southport was scrambling for cash. Maybe that had something to do with Rob McGraw asking me how I was going to pay back $25 million a month ago. But no way was I bringing that subject back up. Details on what was going on were sketchy or non-existent, and tensions were very, very high.

It was not a good time to waltz into the office from the "vineyard" asking for money.

But what choice did I have?

Thursday, January 30, 2014

I have a meeting with Alex scheduled at 11:30 am. As usual, I'm early, but even earlier than on most occasions. I'd found that if I left the vineyard at 8:00 am, I'd be on the dreaded Long Island Expressway by 8:30. That would usually give me an hour before I hit traffic in the western part of Nassau County… if I was lucky.

The ride from Nassau County through Queens to the Mid-Town Tunnel could be another hour. Or more. Then you have to deal with midtown Manhattan.

I love driving in Manhattan. My vision, hearing, thinking, and body all are on super high-alert. There's an exhilaration to it. Maybe I should have been a cabbie or Uber driver.

I showed up at Southport Lane's offices almost an hour early. The traffic gods were good to me. I sat and talked to Jeff for a few moments. Then I set myself up in my usual spot—the small conference room next to Alex's office. It was a great position from which to observe the goings-on in the office.

It was clear that something was up. Alex, Andrew, Rob, Hugh, and some of the insurance guys were behind closed doors in Alex's office. When that confab ended, the insurance guys all moved back to their section of the office while the rest moved to Andrew's office, where they continued to meet.

No one sat down. They stood, huddled closely together behind closed doors. But it looked like they were whispering. Every now and then, the conversations appeared to grow heated. You could tell by their gesticulations. Now, I couldn't hear a thing. But I do remember Rob being the most animated of the participants. That was odd too. Rob was a quiet, reserved guy.

Something was up.

At around 11:25 am, I picked up my computer, stuffed it into my backpack, and ambled toward the big conference room. Jeff asked me if he wanted me to join the meeting. I told him I was asking for money.

Always a survivor, Jeff said he would pass.

The vineyard would need about $250,000 to get through the slow winter months. In late January, though, things are about as slow as they get. Our expense structure remains bloated. Some folks have also figured out that if you appeal to Alex's ego, you nearly always get your way. That didn't help.

For example, early the previous year, someone had convinced Alex that we needed a tasting room in the uber-rich Hamptons.

So, what did they do? They leased a spot in the oh-so-fashionable town of East Hampton for 10 years at $10,000 per month. But there was no liquor license for the location, which you obviously need to open a wine bar. So Southport ran up huge legal fees trying every trick in the book to get a liquor license, including putting the application to the state in some corporate name. That's a no-no. The lawyer should have known better. But what did he care? He was billing around $600 an hour.

By summer's end in 2013, they'd already sunk $138,682 into this little bit of foolishness—construction and design costs. But that wasn't the end of it.

In 2014, the site was finally granted a liquor license. A few months later, we received a zoning notice violation from the town. It seems the building was not zoned for liquor service. Something that should have been known before they signed the lease, don't you think?

Great lawyering, huh?

So, Southport spent hundreds of thousands of dollars to set up a wine bar in a building not zoned to be any type of bar, let alone a wine bar. To add insult to injury, the location didn't generate enough revenue to cover the rent in the summer of 2014.

First chance I had, I shut the place down and moved everything out. Then I fired the idiot lawyer I'd inherited. Be careful. He now teaches law, further proving that those who can't do… teach.

With a new lawyer, I settled the lawsuits from the town and the landlord.

As I sat in the conference room waiting for Alex, I knew this was a make-or-break meeting for the vineyard. Without financial support, I didn't see how we would make it a month.

CFO Dave, Ami, and I had worked out a budget proposal. Dave put it together on a spreadsheet. We went over it again and again. Then I made three or four copies to hand out at this meeting.

Alex was about ten minutes late for our meeting. As usual, I was looking at my watch. I wanted to be back through the Mid-Town Tunnel before 2:00 pm.

He walked into the conference room in much the same manner as he did on the very first day I'd met him. But he was looking a lot worse for wear than the last time I'd seen him at the house a month ago, even though he was drunk and high then.

He sat down, but he never stopped looking at his phone. Reading and typing, he was a study in distraction. He only picked his head up when I slid our spreadsheet over to him.

He looked down at it, got to the bottom line, and said, "Jesus, Richard! You gotta stop losing money like this."

"Then let me cut this place down, Alex," I snapped. "There's way too much bloat for a little company like this." I didn't mention his girlfriend's best pal on the payroll, the East Hampton foolishness, or a host of other absurdities.

Alex shrunk back in his seat and resumed looking at his phone. He was now paying no attention to me.

Suddenly and without taking his eyes off the screen, he said, "Oh fuck, oh fuck, oh fuck!"

I don't know what happened or what he was reading. I still don't. But in that instant, I was actually concerned for him. He wasn't much older than my oldest son.

"You okay, kid?" I asked.

He sat there quietly for a moment and said, "I hate my insurance companies."

He then got up out of his chair and walked to the elevators. No "goodbye," no "I'll be right back." Nothing. A moment later, the door closed on the elevator he was in. That was it.

I never saw or spoke to him again.

CHAPTER 30

After Alex Burns walked out, I sat there alone in the conference room for something like 15 to 20 minutes. Was he coming back?

What had just happened?

I mean, the poor manners he demonstrated by getting up and walking out— I couldn't fathom them. I'd like to think of myself as polite, perhaps to a fault. I can't imagine ever doing something like that to someone, no matter how stressful the moment.

I like to think I'd say "Thank you, sir," even to the guy giving me the blindfold and cigarette in front of the firing squad... if I was guilty.

If I wasn't, I like to think I'd start a brawl.

So, I waited. Politely. I just sat there. No one came in to tell me anything. No one wanted to know where Alex was. Nothing. I sat there as people streamed out of the office to go find lunch somewhere. No one even looked my way. They all walked out and left.

After about 20 minutes, I packed up and walked out too.

The good news was, I'd make it through the Mid-Town Tunnel nice and early. That meant I'd be back to the North Fork and the vineyard before the end of the business day. It also meant I could have dinner at A Touch of Venice in Cutchogue—my favorite restaurant.

But the bad news was... I still had no idea how I was going to keep the vineyard alive through the next month... let alone till the summer busy season kicked in.

A week later, Jeff called me. It sounded like he had his hands over the phone trying to muffle his voice.

Nothing was ever the same after this phone call... ever.

"Hey... no one outside the office knows this. But Alex Burns checked into Bellevue last week. He resigned from Southport and gave all his ownership to Andrew as long as Southport wouldn't sue him."

What? Huh?

Okay. Let me explain what immediately flashed through my mind.

For those of us who grew up in the New York metropolitan area, one thing was sure: Bellevue was a euphemism for the psychiatric ward. Or worse, their emergency room.

No one in their right mind went to Bellevue voluntarily.

Grace Healy is a cousin on my mother's side. Her father (my mother's uncle) Morgan Healy was a New York cop. He made it to captain. He died on the job. My father always said, "That was some funeral they had for him!"

Anyway, Grace was a nurse in the Bellevue Emergency Room in the 1970s and 1980s. She's a tiny little thing with an unrestrained Irish temperament. She probably pulled hundreds if not thousands of knives and bullets out of people. She's fearless. After about 20 years, she quit nursing and went to law school before moving to Seattle. Then she moved back to New York. That was no surprise. She's a total "New Yawka."

A proud product of Jackson Heights, Queens, she was tough as nails and a dedicated Yankees fan. But when there was a death on that side of the family, you knew you were in for a fun night. I made it a point to hang out with Grace and her brothers Morgan, Jr, and Jimmy. After the wake and the night before a funeral, we always wound up at a great Irish bar, usually in Astoria, Queens. There would be lots of drinks and a raft of stories to tell. Some of which may actually have been true!

So, when Jeff merely mentioned Bellevue to me, that meant something bad. Bad for Alex. Bad for me. And bad for the 43 employees who worked at Lieb Cellars, Lieb Vineyards, and Premium Wine Group. Alex was the only person at Southport who gave a damn about the vineyard. Nobody else cared, unless they wanted some free wine or to use the house some weekend. But the business side? They wanted nothing to do with the vineyard.

I had a lot to think about, starting with: How do I keep the vineyard alive now? But more important, what was going on at Southport without Alex?

It was shortly before Valentine's Day, the day which marks the beginning of the long, slow revival of the high-margin, retail wine business. Slowly but surely, the walk-in traffic in the tasting rooms would begin to pick up.

But it would be months before you stop worrying that you would cover payroll with any confidence. The way I saw it, I had two ways to keep the place alive.

First, I could tap into Premium Wine Group's positive cash flow. But that was dangerous. Premium was the goose that laid the golden egg. If I tapped in too hard and hurt Premium, that could be fatal all around, especially for me. I'd be defending myself in court for years to come.

Second, I could put my own money in to bridge cash flow gaps. Say we needed money to cover payroll on Friday. I'm an analyst by nature. So, I figured out pretty quickly—I actually developed a financial model that helped me become adept at predicting—how much cash the tasting rooms would bring in over the weekend.

So, every two weeks, I'd wire from my personal account about 75 percent of the estimated weekend's revenue. That would generally cover the gross payroll costs. When the Lieb wine money came in, I'd pay myself back.

Oh yeah, the interest charge for my little private lending facility? Zero.

Why? If things went to hell in a handbasket, I didn't want some creditor's lawyer accusing me of anything sinister or predatory. I also insisted the CFO keep his own ledger for this activity. I wanted to be able to produce a second-party confirmation at a moment's notice if anyone—lawyers, regulators, whoever—requested it.

The truth is that for the next four years, this is how we survived. It was a constant high-wire act. But I had no choice. I had to keep these companies alive.

I also skipped a lot of my own paychecks in the winter months, hoping to catch up on the missed checks during the busy season. That worked too. But only because I controlled the checking accounts for all the companies.

But if Alex was truly out of the picture, that meant I could cut costs without pushback from him. So, I did. With fervor.

Alex's girlfriend's bestie read the writing on the wall. She quit. Hell, she probably knew better than anyone else what was going on with Alex.

I still had a hard time believing Alex was truly gone. I was waiting for him to show up at the vineyard any day, as if nothing had happened. He never did.

Ami, Russell, CFO Dave, and I now began taking a hard look at every aspect of Lieb's operation. The only way I was going to get everyone through this difficult time was by being open and transparent about everything. Every financial detail, every personnel change, every relationship, every problem… everything was on the table at our weekly meetings.

Well almost everything.

I knew instinctively that there was no value to letting them in on all the details I termed in my head as "Southport Shit." By that I mean my deep suspicions that there was a crime involved here.

But I had no proof. Why make their burden worse? So, I did my best to keep them focused solely on the vineyard.

But in the next 60 days, we cut nearly $40,000 out of the monthly payroll at Lieb.

In a counter-intuitive move—that's a nice way of saying it could be either exceedingly stupid or disastrous—we got rid of nearly all our sales force. Instead of paying our salesforce to sell, or not sell, as was the case for several of them, we decided to audition wholesale distributors who would do the selling for us.

All we did was sell to them at an agreed-upon discount. In other words, our wholesale price. It took two years to work out. But when it finally bore fruit, we grew like mad.

Our winemaker, Russell Hearn, is the genius behind Premium Wine Group. Premium's position in the industry gave Russell unparalleled insight into the local market. Russell knows where every pound of grapes and every gallon of wine is on the North Fork.

Russell understood the situation we were in. Let's face it, it was in his self-interest to know. He wanted to shield Premium from being sucked under by Lieb. So, he offered a brilliant idea, at least to me, because I didn't know you could do this. "How about if we sold our excess grape production?" he suggested. "We grew way more grapes than we needed for next year's vintage." Sometimes, the most brilliant ideas are the simplest. Like this one.

I asked Russell why it hadn't been done in the past. He told me that the old owners and then Alex Burns wouldn't allow it.

Well, I sure as hell would. I even offered to pay him a 10 percent commission, which he gladly accepted. I didn't care. We needed the money. We had to get to the summertime. Then I'd have some breathing room to figure out how we were going to make it through the following winter.

There was no guarantee any of this would work. I woke up many a night doing the numbers in my head, hoping they showed a path to the summer. Forget that! Most of the time I was just trying to get to Friday.

But what haunted me throughout was the fact that 43 people depended on me. They had lives outside of work. They had husbands, they had wives, they had children, they had mortgages. I didn't want to be the one to tell them that they were out of a job, and everything in their lives was now in jeopardy, because of some idiots at a fake private equity firm in Manhattan.

My biggest fear was the conversation that began: "You have no job."

I mean, I'd done it before. When I was running the steel company in Los Angeles, I laid off over 100 people in one day. It sucked more than you can ever imagine.

Making it even more horrible, I walked into a Chinese restaurant a few months post-layoffs to pick up takeout for a family dinner. Grabbed a seat at the bar, looked up… and the bartender is someone I laid off a couple months before. I tried to apologize. But he didn't care.

It's the worst feeling you can imagine. It never leaves you. It still hasn't.

You never want to repeat that. At all. Ever.

So, I was determined to survive. No matter what I had to do.

***

About a week after Alex disappeared, I received the following e-mail from Dean, Southport's Comptroller. I didn't know him well. But as Controller, I assumed he knew where all the money was... or wasn't.

At first, I thought it was a joke. But in my brief experience with Dean, he never showed the slightest sense of humor.

From: Dean
Sent: Friday, February 7, 2014, 5:17 PM
To: Richard Bailey

Richard,

I'm trying to gather up some more information on PBEV to get a better understanding of what is in PBEV. I know some time in August, PBEV issued $10mm worth of preferred. What did PBEV receive for this issuance? Does PBEV have its own cash account?

Thanks,
Dean

Ten million dollars? What $10 million?

The Preferred Shares issued last summer were for $1.2 million. Not $10 million.

Since I was never able to get anyone to document the deal, there was no written record or determination of their actual value.

I guess Alex never canceled the stock issuance, as he told me he would a few weeks earlier.

Most important… they had my signature on them!

It only took a couple of seconds for me to realize that this was a problem. A big problem and a very serious legal problem for me personally.

After a great deal of thought, I sent the following e-mail response to Dean the following day:

From: Richard Bailey
Sent: Saturday, February 8, 2014, 3:40 PM
To: Dean

Dean:

Sorry, I just saw this. PBEV issued 10,000 shares of preferred on the orders of Alex in early to mid-August 2013. It happened simultaneously with my being told I was a member of the SLND (precursor to PBEV) board of directors. When I asked Alex what was the consideration SLND was receiving for the shares, he told me it was for the monies put into the vineyard over and above the purchase price by PWA, which at that point was approximately $1.2 million.

Later (around October), when I asked him about the documentation for the preferred—as this would be a 2013 audit item—he told me they were going to be canceled and reissued in smaller lots—he wanted hem listed so they would trade. Again, I asked for documentation.

The next time I brought it up was on December 29, 2013, at the house at Cutchogue as we were expecting PBEV to acquire the Lieb entities imminently. He then told me that he was going to cancel the preferred altogether.

PBEV does not have a cash account. David and I were going to set one up once the acquisition of the Lieb entities by PBEV was complete.

RDB

Richard D. Bailey
President & Chief Executive Officer
Premium Beverage Group Inc.
PO Box 907
Cutchogue, NY 11935

***

What was going on at Southport? My signature was on a piece of paper that may have been forged by someone. So, I had to get my side placed into the written record… now. As my friend Brad likes to say, "The truth is the easiest thing to remember." So that's what I gave them.

From that point on, everything changed. I didn't know (and still don't) how $1.2 million in Preferred Stock had suddenly become $10 million. But I knew I needed a lawyer. No way was I using Southport's. They represented Southport, not me.

I didn't have hard evidence of criminal wrongdoing. But now I highly suspected it. Here's what I had which fueled my suspicion:

1. I had bank statements showing money going out in all sorts of unorthodox transfers.

2. That same bank account was intentionally hidden from public company auditors.

3. Rob McGraw was asking how I was going to pay back the $25 million that the vineyard owed even though I had no record of it being owed.

4. Southport's majority owner got up and walked out, only to check himself into Bellevue's psych ward. He then relinquished all his ownership in exchange for not being sued. Anyone remember Jeff Skilling and Enron in 2001? How'd that work out?

5. Finally, I had my signature on a $1.2 million Preferred Stock issuance that someone has been tricked into believing was worth $10 million.

Even though I was still on Southport's payroll, I no longer viewed anyone at Southport as a friend other than Jeff. Everyone else were potential adversaries. And I harbored no illusions that they would defend me. They wouldn't. They would throw me under the bus in a heartbeat if it was in their best interests. They were those type of guys.

I needed a lawyer. A really good lawyer.

CHAPTER 31

Three Months Later
May 2014

After Alex Burns' sudden and mysterious departure, everything changed. I mean *everything*.

The beginning of May 2014 would be my one-year anniversary at Southport and the vineyard. On the last day of April, Andrew Scherr called to tell me that Southport could no longer afford to pay me.

So, he laid me off.

He did tell me that if I wanted to keep getting get paid, I was going to have to find the money at the vineyard. "But," he said, "I don't blame you if you quit."

Bob Yingling, the CFO, told me a month earlier, "We're just waiting for the liquidators to walk in."

As a living, breathing business. Southport had ceased to exist.

See, when an owner of an insurance company—like Alex—resigns and commits himself to a psychiatric hospital… well, that causes all sorts of problems. Insurance companies are not like normal companies. They're tightly regulated. Ownership changes must be approved by state regulators. Sudden ownership changes give regulators heartburn.

So when Alex checked out of Southport and into Bellevue, he set off a chain of events no one at Southport could stop. It was truly the beginning of the end of Southport Lane.

In early March, I learned that Freestone Insurance hired an outside examiner to review it. They hired Duff & Phelps, a well-respected firm specializing in securities valuations. Duff & Phelps were known for conducting thorough examinations.

Duff & Phelps also wanted to speak with the management of

Southport's portfolio companies. They needed to understand what Southport owned and what it was worth. By that time, there were about 10-11 investments in the private equity portfolio.

So out of nearly a dozen private equity portfolio companies, Southport produced only one manager to speak with Duff & Phelps.

Me.

Dave, PBEV's CFO, and I prepared budgets and projections for the call. Southport needed to show the examiners how we intended to make money in the years ahead.

I was also under strict orders from Southport to "be positive." Kind of tough to do. The vineyard was in a deep financial hole.

The call took place on March 28, 2014. It was excruciating.

Southport e-mailed me the documents a few minutes before the call. Included were the budgets and projections Dave and I had prepared.

A few minutes into the interview, I saw a problem. The spreadsheets provided to Duff & Phelps were not the ones Dave and I had prepared. The projections showed strong profitability far earlier than Dave and I forecast. It was clear someone at Southport had "dummied up" the projections. By dummied up, I mean someone changed them to make the future look like sunshine, roses, and breezy days at the beach. Not what Dave and I had estimated.

So I spent the balance of the call answering what I could and replying "I don't know" to much of the rest. I must have sounded like either an idiot or a co-conspirator. Like I was hiding something.

I was furious. How could they do this and just spring it on me? What were they thinking? Did they think I didn't recognize my own projections? Did they think I'd just roll over and play along?

I got off the phone feeling deeply betrayed. And that goes nowhere good.

Now, I don't get really, really mad very often. But when I do, I seethe. For hours. For days. I don't talk much. I don't put it behind me. I don't move on. I can't. No matter who tells me to. No matter how often they tell me.

I obsess over it. I've got to think it out. I've got to think about every…single… permutation. Then I've got to think out each permutation of each permutation. My mother says I "stew" on things. She's right. Mothers usually are.

At some point in this process, I formulate a plan of action. Once I have one, I calm down. But I do see everything differently as a result.

Now—in my head—I had a plan when it came to Southport. Everything was clear.

Looking back, a smart person would have quit immediately after that call. What Southport had done was a breach of faith so deep, so severe that I knew I could never trust them again. But sometimes I gotta wade into the fight. I've told both my sons—and I truly believe this—there are times when fighting is the most honest thing in the world to do.

So instead of walking away. I wanted to get even. I wanted to see them lose. Everything.

I wanted to fight.

But most importantly, the Duff & Phelps call also confirmed the source of the money used to buy the vineyard.

Freeport Insurance was formerly known as Dallas National Insurance. After buying it, they renamed it and made it a Delaware Corporation. It was the first insurance company Southport purchased. Right after they gained control of Freestone's cash, they purchased the vineyard.

A simple Google search showed me that. It was easy. Befitting Alex's ego, his PR firm put out press release announcing the Freestone deal.

On April 28th—one month after the Duff & Phelps call—my Google news feed popped up with an alert on Freestone Insurance.

The Insurance Commissioner for the State of Delaware had posted an order on their website. Freestone was now under the protection of the State of Delaware. The order was issued under the authority of the Delaware Chancery Court.

Now, for the super secretive dealmakers at Southport, that was the worst development of all. They were going to have to explain themselves... to regulators. Maybe even law enforcement.

I wanted to see them slowly roast on a spit over an open fire. This was going to be fun.

The busy summer season was right in front of us. The tasting rooms were busy. The spring bottling season was drawing to a close at Premium Wine Group. Russell had sold off about $100,000 of grapes we would harvest in the fall. We were generating cash from multiple fronts every day. What a difference from January through March.

Cash flow was less of a worry. I began to pay myself back the money I'd lent over the winter. I arranged to get paid 50 percent of my salary at Lieb and 50 percent at Premium. That seemed fair to me.

I'd also learned that I *liked* this business. I liked the rhythms to it. I liked the people. I liked being out on the North Fork of Long Island. I liked the ferry rides each week. I even liked the agricultural aspects. Which is odd because the closest I ever came to a farm growing up was driving past one.

As I began my second busy season at the vineyard, we had some financial breathing room. Not a lot. And not for long. But I'd learned a lot of lessons about how the cash flows worked in the wine industry. I didn't know how we were going to make it through next winter. But I had time to figure that out.

But Southport was never far from my mind.

I've spent almost 30 years toiling in the world of corporate finance. I've bought companies from and sold companies to global giants. I've tried to fix small businesses that were in trouble. I've done work with big and small private equity firms. All those firms operated in tried-and-true, predictable fashion.

But nothing at Southport Lane was predictable. Ever.

I still could not get my head around how three or four ordinary guys wound up with control of four or five insurance companies.

Jeff and I talked about it all the time. He had left Southport in the spring. Smart move. He knew the insurance companies had financial problems. But he didn't know how bad they were.

Brad and I talked about it a ton. We still couldn't figure it out. We had theories but no proof. Where did the money come from to buy these insurance companies? It was a complete mystery.

One night, I went down a rabbit hole on the website of the Securities and Exchange Commission. Sitting alone at the vineyard house, I came across something interesting.

On October 1, 2012, the Destra Targeted Income Unit Investment Trust filed Form N-8B-2 with the SEC. It was available on the EDGAR (Electronic Data Gathering and Reporting) website. Edgar makes available forms filed by companies and others required by law to file with the SEC. It's a terrific database and service.

Buried deep in the filing was a reference to "a loan agreement relating to senior debt securities issued by Premium Wine Acquisition, LLC."

But there was a problem. Premium Wine Acquisitions had no debt. What they did have was stock in Premium Beverage Group… which had no debt. They also had a lot of other funky money movements.

Then I realized… this must the $25 million Rob McGraw had referred to back in December.

After you file a document with the SEC, you best do exactly what you said in the document you were going to do. If you don't, it's called securities fraud. Now, I know where all $18 million of the $25 million went.

After all, I had the bank statements.

Knowing Southport as I now do, I'll bet they have violated the use of funds specified in this document over and over and over.

If I can prove it, I've got the first nail in their coffin.

In late July 2014, I received an alert on my Google news feed. It was another decision of the Delaware Chancery Court. On August 15, 2014, the State Insurance Commissioner would seize Freestone Insurance. Then… it would liquidate it.

I knew, at that moment, that I was free of Southport. The only problem is Southport didn't know that I knew that. They acted like nothing had changed.

The reality was that Southport could make a claim to own PBEV. But they'd lose. Based upon the Chancery Court ruling, I could tie Southport up in court for years. In the meantime, I'd be completely in charge.

Perfect.

All I needed to do was make the argument that the money used to buy the vineyard was from the Destra Unit Investment Trust. And if the Unit Investment Trusts were sold to Freestone, then I was free from Southport.

But it also meant I now worked for the State of Delaware's Insurance Commissioner. It was then that my lawyer began a long effort to try and contact the representatives of the Insurance Commissioner—an effort that would take more than 18 months.

My relationship with Southport at the time was cordial. On the outside, I displayed no animosity towards them. I hid my contempt and confided in no one except Paul Doherty, my lawyer, as we planned to break free.

Around that same time, I also became hooked on the show "American Greed" on CNBC.

Some nights they would show episode after episode. So, I'd sit there, in the oversized comfy chair in the vineyard house sunroom, a glass of wine nearby and watch "American Greed." For hours. Five to six episodes a night.

The second episode I watched was about a guy named Shalom Weiss.

It seems Shalom—who was from Long Island—got control of an insurance company named National Heritage Life.

In a scheme that could almost have been the template for Southport Lane, Weiss took over National Heritage with money he didn't have.

When National Life was liquidated in 1995, it had about 35,000 policy holders, 10,500 of whom lived in Florida.

Many lost their life savings because of the fraud. By the time he was through, Shalom Weiss had pilfered nearly $450 million from National Heritage.

Weiss was arrested and released on bail. He rejected a guilty plea which would have sent him to prison for five years. He decided to go to trial.

In 1999, while the jury was deliberating, Weiss fled the country. He was found guilty despite his absence, then arrested overseas and brought back.

Shalom Weiss was sentenced to 845 years in prison. The longest prison sentence ever given to a white-collar criminal.

When American Greed finally revealed the sentence, I spit out a mouthful of red wine all over the upholstery of that nice white chair.

That was all I needed to know.

CHAPTER 32

October 2014

Now what do I do?

I'm pretty convinced Southport has committed a crime or two or three, if not more. But I'm not a lawyer, so I'm not sure.

When I don't understand something, I usually step back and outline it all on paper. I admit, I'm either old-fashioned or had way too much Catholic education (grammar school, college, and graduate school).

But when I can't figure something out, I try to find the syllogism in my thinking. Undergoing this exercise gives me clarity.

You know...

- If A=B
- And B=C
- Then A=C

If I can find a syllogism which supports my thinking, great. If not, I keep searching.

Anyway, it's the way my brain works. I can't help it. I know it pisses people off. But I cannot think of a better way to examine the past 18 months of shenanigans at Southport Lane.

From the beginning, there had been a steady sequence of oddball, out-of-the-ordinary events. One or two I can explain away. Different people do things in different ways. But at Southport, there were so much that was out of the ordinary. So much that made little or no sense. I was sure that there had to be a connecting theme.

So, I broke the argument down into hard evidence and soft evidence. Hard evidence usually wins the day in legal matters. Remember, my brother Tom told me: "The written record is the case in litigation."

So, I had:

Hard Evidence

- A full years' worth of bank statements.
- A breakdown and classification of every dollar spent according to those statements.
- A copy of Form N-8B-2 filed by Destra Capital Management—whoever they were—which showed where the money came from.
- A preferred stock issuance for $1.2 million, which was then sold to an insurance company as being worth $10 million.

But soft evidence is what wakes you up at night.

Soft Evidence

- Alex Burns: A founder who lies without concern about detection.
- A company that conceals the existence of a critical checking account from public company auditors. In other words, two sets of books.
- A $3 million set of expenditures described as "Shit I Did."
- Raubritter translates to "Robber Baron." Okay, maybe a bad joke. But not one to be made by someone who wants other financial professionals to take him seriously.
- The acquisition of a vineyard at over twice its value, in cash! Okay, that just may be stupid. But my experience with private equity guys is that they're not stupid. In fact, most try to squeeze the last dollar out of every deal. Overpay? Very rare. Underpay? A cherished goal.
- Alex Burns walks out of a meeting and checks himself into a Bellevue psychiatric ward. He then renounces all

interest in the company he founded when that company agrees not to sue him.

So, it stands to reason that Southport lied to the SEC and to the various insurance companies.

***

So here's the syllogism I came up with:

- IF Southport lied to insurance companies and the Securities Exchange Commission…
- AND if lying to insurance companies and the SEC is an act of fraud, which it is…
- THEN Southport committed fraud.

This was no longer a stretch of the imagination. It was plain, simple, and clear: Southport committed fraud.

Even more frightening, it seemed like everyone working there was doing their best to cover it up.

Now, to be honest, the folks at Southport were never apostles of full disclosure anyway. You never got the full story from any of them. Ever. They only told you what they needed you to know.

Everyone knew the situation was tense. So, it may have been that they all were super cautious when they spoke to you. But even then, you got off the phone and usually had doubts about what you'd just heard.

See, when Alex was still involved, people shrugged the odd things off with the roll of the eyes and a simple "ask Alex." They were all afraid the little boy in the "Twilight Zone" episode would ostracize them to the cornfield. Nobody wanted to risk their jobs.

I admit, I didn't want to risk mine, either. Alex was an unguided missile.

But after Alex left, the Southport powers that be circled the wagons, joined hands, and said in unison: "Alex did it. We had no knowledge of any of that." They even tried for a moment to blame it on my buddy Jeff. That was another load of lies.

As my son Alex said in the fall of 2013, "Bull Fucking Shit." They knew. They all knew. They just lied.

If it wasn't true, then Alex Burns had a complete and separate firm doing things behind the backs of everyone at Southport. Put another way, this phantom firm was doing it all in the name of Southport, and none of these guys knew. What a crock of shit!

No one believed it. But they stuck to it.

But I had the bank statements and the document filed with the SEC. I knew where the money came from. I knew where the money went. I knew which insurance company put up the cash. I knew that Duff & Phelps was crawling all over Southport. I also knew that someone at Southport had altered PBEV's financial projections. Yeah, that still stung.

I was certain there was at least a $25 million fraud here. Was it civil? Was it criminal? I didn't know. But somebody clearly had done some bad shit.

So, what do you do when you have evidence of a crime by your employer? Definitely not what you see in the movies. You don't get all "Norma Rae" full of righteous indignation. You don't feel like some warrior for justice. You get scared. At least I did.

I also went into a series of deep conversations with myself. Call it my conscience. Call it what you will. But for me it was some heavy-duty examination of the facts and the consequences. All competed with the voice in the back of my head saying, "Who died and made you boss?"

You also weigh all those things against the consequences if you're wrong.

On the one hand, I didn't want to be a part of what I feared was a criminal enterprise. I don't ever want to be in that position. I actually care what people think of me. I want my family, especially my parents, wife, and two sons to be proud of me. Tough to do when you're committing fraud.

But I was struggling. The best I could tell, Southport still claimed to own 92 percent of the stock of PBEV. I was their appointed Chief Executive Officer. I liked the business. I was *very well* paid. I liked the people I worked with at the vineyard. It was the type of job people dream about for their retirement. Run a vineyard? It's a nice fucking gig.

But what if I turn them in, and then find out I'm wrong? The only information I had was vineyard-related. They'd know it was me in a heartbeat.

Oh and forget all that stuff about whistleblowers and whistleblower protections. I had no faith that any of that would help me. I didn't even know where to start with that stuff.

But what if I was right and did nothing? The argument in my head about profiting from ill-gotten gains: That was unpleasant.

Maybe no one will notice, I thought, and they would leave PBEV alone.

Yeah right. Alex paid $12.75 million in cash for something worth around $6.0 million. The likelihood that won't attract attention is zero.

I knew there would be a knock on the door someday. Even if it was only lawyers serving lawsuits. But I wanted nothing to do with that.

So I made the decision. I wanted to be on the right side of what I suspected was a very ugly story.

Experience tells me that it's better to be proactive than reactive. Better to be part of the solution than lumped in as part of the problem.

But going to law enforcement? I'd been in some nasty jams in my career, but I'd never initiated a criminal investigation.

CHAPTER 33

Seven houses down from us lives my neighbor Donnie. Donnie is one of the world's good guys. Our kids are similar ages and have gone to the same schools. So, I saw Donnie at all sorts of school events over the years.

I always saw Donnie at my next-door neighbor's annual St. Patrick's Day bashes. He was always good for a laugh or a funny conversation.

Earlier that year, my son Alex was home for semester break. It was his freshman year in college. So we walked next door to the annual St Paddy's Day party. There would easily be 50 adults, and some years at least that many kids.

When Donnie walked into the party, he saw my son Alex and made a beeline for him. In his baritone voice and deep *Bahhston* accent, he said, "Hey Alex, congratulations on getting into Yale. We're proud of you. The whole neighborhood is proud of you. You made the property values go up!"

All the adults in the room broke up laughing. Alex and the other boys looked a little spooked.

Donnie is an FBI agent. All the kids knew that. Donnie made teenage boys nervous.

Me? I thought he was hot shit.

***

Every Sunday, I go to the dump. Oh, excuse me, the "Transfer Station." It's where we drop off our household trash. Where we separate our plastics from our cardboard. Our cans from our bottles. Our food trash from everything else. Then we drop them into huge bins, which are then carted off to who knows? Probably an incinerator somewhere.

145

In our part of Massachusetts, recycling isn't a chore. It's a civic obligation, right alongside one's duty to vote. You see more people at the transfer station on Sunday than at Mass.

It's also where you run into all sorts of people in town. Local celebrities during the summer. Politicians running for office in the fall. Your neighbors at any time of the year.

It's Sunday, October 19, 2014. The transfer station is usually packed on Sunday morning. But it really depends on what time the Patriots are playing.

On this particular Sunday, I loaded up my car and drove over to the transfer station. Once there, I got in line behind 30 to 40 other cars looking to do the same thing.

First you go to the recycling section. I dropped off our bottles, our plastics, our cans, and our cardboard products in the proper bins.

Then I hopped back in the car and drove over to drop off the regular household garbage, which is in nice blue bags. The town sells you the nice blue bags, just so you can throw them away.

I hopped out of the car, grabbed the blue bag in the back, and chucked it into the bin. When I turned around, there was Donnie, our neighborhood FBI agent not 10 feet away from me.

Always friendly, Donnie calls out, "Hey! How you doing, man?"

I didn't intend to do it. But I just let it out. In fact, I was surprised to hear myself say it, "Hey, I think I need to talk business with you."

"What's the mattah? You in trouble?" he says. He's no longer smiling.

"No," I say. "But I think my employer is."

I then gave him a 30-second synopsis of the Southport story as I knew it.

When I finished, he looked at me and said, "Give me your numbah. I'm gonna call one of our white-collar guys. We can have breakfast together tomorrow and talk this out."

By the time I got home fewer than 15 minutes later, Donnie had texted me the time and location.

"8:00 am. Tomorrow. Jamie's."

***

I spent the next several hours asking myself, "What the fuck did I just do?" I berated myself, over and over. All Donnie asked was how I was doing. And how did I respond? I blurted out everything like a scared little kid.

The rest of the day was a waste. Forget all the bullshit about feeling like you got a weight off your shoulders. There was no feeling of serenity and calm after talking to Donnie. Just anxiety. In epic proportions.

So, I spent the afternoon lurching between kicking myself and justifying myself. Between saying, "Well, that was a half-assed move" to "someone has to do this."

But I also spent the afternoon and evening preparing. I printed out the excel spread sheet which detailed where the money went. But I also had the original one with Alex Burns' handwritten "S.I.D" next to where the $3 million went out the side door. I printed out a complete copy of the Form N-8B-2 filed by Destra Capital Management.

I sketched out a flow chart showing how the Freestone money traveled to its various recipients.

When I walked into that breakfast the next morning, I wanted to have the facts right there with me.

***

I didn't sleep very well that night. No surprise there.

I was grateful for the morning routine. My wife is a teacher. Her alarm goes off at 5:30 am. She's out the door an hour later. But getting our son Reid out the door sometimes took a little extra "coaching," especially during football season, what with homework, lunch money, practice uniform, two pairs of socks, and gym bag, to gather up and take with him each day. Then into the car for the ride to school.

When I got home from dropping Reid off, I showered, shaved, and started to get dressed. I wondered for about ten seconds what you should wear to a secret meeting with the FBI. Then I laughed, called myself an idiot, and put on the same thing I always do: khakis, button-down shirt, sneakers, fleece jacket.

Jamie's is no more than a mile and a half from my house. It would take me less than five minutes to get there. So I sat, waited, and got nervous all over again.

Finally, I walked into Jaimie's. There was Donnie and his colleague. I walked over and shook Donnie's hand. As I sat down, he introduced me to Elliot (*not his real name. The FBI agents I dealt with requested that their real names not be used*). Elliot specialized in white-collar crime.

Over the course of the next 30 minutes, I outlined on a notepad the money sources and the money flow. I walked them through the unique personalities involved. I showed them my documentation, including the "Shit I Did" sheet.

When I was through, Donnie looked over at Elliot and asked, "What do you think?"

"There are all the markings and characteristics of a major fraud here," Elliot said.

Donnie got up. He was still working the Boston Marathon bombing case. He looked at Elliot and said, "It's all yours."

Donnie looked at me and said, "Everybody here knows me. They know who I work for. I don't want them to see me and you together and think you're in trouble. So I'm going to leave you two here."

Then, looking directly at me with his FBI game face on, he said sternly, "You need anything, you got my numbah. Call me. I'm just down the street."

Elliot and I chatted for a few more minutes. He explained to me what would happen next, then told me to sit tight until I heard from him.

***

I didn't hear from Elliott for several months. During that stretch, every time I drove by his house, I looked for Donnie. I was hoping I could stop by and get an impromptu update. But I never saw him.

Having handed over incriminating evidence, I thought the FBI would call me within a few weeks. Southport had pulled off some complex transactions. Maybe I could help explain them or give context to them.

But I heard nothing.

Then *The Wall Street Journal* got hold of the story.

CHAPTER 34

For someone like me, running a business is all about goals and communication. Ask Ami or Russell or anyone at the vineyard who reported to me. First rule: Get everyone on board with the goals and how they get there. Second rule: Communicate, communicate, communicate. Communication is everything. Businesses run better when everyone knows what everyone else is doing and why they're doing it.

As a leader, I like to give good people clear goals. Make sure they buy into them. Structure their compensation so they know that if they do this, they get that. Then I like to step back and let them do the things they can do better than me. From there, I like to listen, answer questions, and solve problems. Of course, I'm also there to course-correct if they veer off plan.

My job isn't to do their job. My job is to give them the tools which will let them do their jobs to the best of their ability. Then stand back and get out of their way.

But the FBI operates on a whole different set of principles. At least that's what I figured from the position I was in. So, when Elliot said, "Sit tight until you hear from me," that's exactly what I did.

Boy did that suck.

In the meantime, for Lieb Cellars and Premium Wine Group, winter was coming.

The previous winter, after Alex disappeared, I was able to convince Andrew Scherr to wire in $250,000. I made the same presentation to Andrew that I did to Alex on the day he got up and walked out. Andrew, who is polite to the core, was more direct. You never had to worry about him frothing at the mouth and spitting at you like Alex tended to do. Andrew was polite. He always comported himself in a measured, business-like fashion. I still thought he was slightly scary. But at least he was polite.

His answer? "Okay, but this is the last you get. No more. You need to figure this out yourself."

This year was different. Summer 2014 had been good to Lieb Cellars. And by good, I mean that from May through October, we had managed not to lose money. During that same period, Premium Wine Group was very profitable. But not profitable enough to get everyone through the winter.

So, I did something some considered bold, and some considered stupid. I personally guaranteed a $2,000,000 loan using the hard assets of all the companies as collateral.

Now, I didn't have $2,000,000. But by guaranteeing the loan, that ensured I'd be the lender's best friend if the company failed. If they didn't get $2,000,000 from the sale of the assets, then they would sue me for the balance. So, it was in my best interests to help them get the best price possible if we had to sell the assets.

Now, here I need to thank Andrew Scherr and Hugh for something. Both agreed to the loan. It's what saved Lieb Cellars. Without it, I'd have had to shutter Lieb Cellars and focus 100 percent on Premium Wine Group. That would have been an absolute failure in my mind.

But the funny thing was, I didn't really need Southport's approval. The Delaware Insurance Commissioner had taken possession of Freestone Insurance back in August. According to Duff & Phelps, Freestone had an "indirect interest" in the loans made to Premium Wine Acquisition.

On December 30, 2013, PBEV "bought" the vineyard. So, Southport then converted those loans into 92 percent ownership of PBEV. But that also meant the Delaware Insurance Commissioner would be coming for that stock ownership too, eventually.

I didn't need Southport's approval for the loan. But this was not the time to pick that fight. The vineyard and I were still in survival mode.

Andrew called it "a ballsy move." Hugh put it this way, "We're in the asset protection business, not the asset liquidation business." That's all I needed.

Now, I couldn't go to a normal bank for this. How do you explain to a bank that you're not completely sure who owns the company that's borrowing money?

So, after weeks of smile and dial, I found a "hard money lender." The only thing they cared about was whether the company appraised for double the loan value. For that lack of risk management, they charged 12 percent interest. The appraisal value came in at $6,000,000 for a $2,000,000 loan.

If we were in compliance with all the terms of the loan, I was in the clear. I viewed it as an acceptable risk. Shutting down Lieb Cellars would have been disastrous for everyone—the shareholders, whoever they were—the employees, and me.

In late November 2014, we closed on the $2,000,000 loan. I could breathe a little.

We were going to survive. I had several years' worth of cash cushion to fix the business. All I wanted now was for everyone at Southport to back off and let me stabilize and grow the business.

Not a chance with that, though.

***

Shortly after the first of the year, I got a phone call from Hugh. Two reporters from *The Wall Street Journal* were asking questions about Alex. Their names were Leslie Scism and Mark Marmont.

Hugh told me in no uncertain terms that I was not to speak with them. If they did call me, I was to refer them back to Hugh.

I was fine with that. I wanted nothing to do with the press. But I did Google them both. Then I went back and read everything they wrote over the past couple of years.

The Southport story was right up their alley. Young kid. Reckless spending. Unusual transactions. Bellevue. There was so much good material here. Somehow, I didn't think this would be a one-and-done type of article, either. This would be a series. After all, they didn't know the half of it!

It had been nearly a year since Alex walked out of Southport. Apparently, he checked into Bellevue's psychiatric unit, complaining of a "nervous breakdown." He was there for about a day. He then checked out and went home to his mother's house.

What happened after that struck me as weird.

After he left, Alex and Southport signed a separation agreement. In it, they named me responsible for removing Alex's personal effects from the vineyard house.

Within minutes of Hugh telling me about this, I received a call from Alex's mother. I didn't recognize the number, so I let it go to voicemail. Five minutes later, she called again. Five minutes after that, she called a third time. This time I answered.

Boy was she a human tornado. She wanted everything ready and available by the next day. I was to pack up his clothes, toiletries, plates, and dishes he had purchased. Kitchen items. Everything! She also wanted her husband to pick up Alex's Porsche 911 (license plate "REINSURE"). Not to mention his personal wine and cigar collection from the wine cellar in the basement.

I asked her if Alex paid for these items with his money or Southport's. That didn't go over well. But we agreed I'd put his personal items in the Porsche. She could make arrangements to pick it up.

While packing, I found a lot of prescription drugs: Vicodin, Percocet, that kind of stuff, all prescribed by different doctors in Manhattan. What bothered me was that it wasn't one pill jar for each type of drug. It was several pill jars of the same drug from different doctors and pharmacies. They were all full or only partially depleted. That has always bothered me.

Anyway, I refused to give up the cigars and wine collection. I said I needed proof these weren't purchased with "ill-gotten gains." As time went on, the cigars and wine became a bigger problem than they were worth. I had to put a combination lock on the wine-cellar door to keep folks from thinking that the contents inside were party favors. After all, I was the custodian of all this crap. We had inventoried everything and sent that to Southport. Anything and everything could come back to bite me.

But thank God the reporters from *The Wall Street Journal* never contacted me. I was so relieved.

On March 15, 2014, the story broke on the front page of *The Wall Street Journal*. The headline blared:

Young Financier's Insurance Empire Collapses

Investments of insurance companies owned by Southport
Lane Management were swapped for unusual and
sometimes worthless assets

Well, that got your attention. Thank God it was a quiet Saturday morning.

Once again, everything had changed. I gave my employees the heads up and then sat them down and told them "most" of the Southport saga. You could see the worry in their eyes.

"In moments like this," I told our managers, "you can ask me anything. I'll give you the straight scoop."

I never got close to telling them about the FBI and the criminal stuff.

***

To make matters worse, a few weeks before, those Preferred Stock shares had come back to haunt me.

It started when I received the following e-mail from Rob Mc-Graw.

> Richard,
>
> I hope all is well. Below you'll find a request from US Bank to re-register the holders of the PBEV Preferred Securities (issued initially circa Aug 2013 and traded by Alex circa Jan 2014). Let me know when you might have a convenient moment to discuss.
>
> Many thanks.
>
> Regards,
>
> —Robert
>
> In regards to the registrations for Solar Night-Premium Beverage certificates, we would need to have new certificates under the surviving company name indicating the appropriate owners and value as follows:
>
> $7,750,000—Companion-Redwood—15, 500 shares in the name of Blue Cross Blue Shield of South Carolina
>
> $2,250,000—Imperial Management—4,500 shares in

the name of Imperial Management.

Upon receipt of the new certificates, we will cancel the current certificate and provide it to you for your records.

Yikes! Not only did they want me to reissue the Preferred Shares, they wanted me to issue them at the inflated value—the *fraudulent value*—of $10 million. Only problem was they had already been issued for $1.2 million. No $10 million transaction ever took place! So, I ain't signing anything stating they were worth $10 million. No way.

And where the fuck was the FBI? I'd given them all the information on the preferred shares when we met four months ago!

Now what do I do?

***

A few days after the article came out, I was driving by my neighbor Donnie's house. It was a warm late winter day. Finally, I saw him outside. He was doing some cleanup yard work.

I pulled up the cul-de-sac where he lived. His daughter was with him. He saw the look on my face and asked his daughter to go inside.

"Do you have any idea what's going on with Elliot?" I asked.

"No. I'm not in that loop, I'm still working the marathon bombing. Why?" he responded.

"There was a front-page article in *The Wall Street Journal* about this. They say there may be as much as $250 million involved."

"Where's Elliot on that figure?" Donnie asked.

"I haven't heard a word from him since our meeting last October."

Donnie suddenly had his business face on. He looked at me and said, "Go home. Keep your phone close. You'll get a call within the next few minutes."

Damn if he wasn't right. About ten minutes later, my phone rang. It was Elliot.

"Can you come into our office tomorrow? Bring everything you've got on this."

"Absolutely," I respond.

He gave me the time and the address. My wife looked at me and asked me if I was alright. "Yeah, I'm… Just some stupid stuff at the vineyard I have to deal with."

I'm pretty sure she knew I was lying.

**

The old FBI office in Boston is kind of a dump. It was designed by a famous Harvard architect. To me, it looked like a truly ugly, post-Stalin, Soviet designed apartment building.

To get in, you go through multiple security checks, including a metal detector. You hand over your cell phone and your driver's license, which they keep until you leave. They photograph you. Then they search your briefcase or, in my case, my backpack.

After all that was done, I was escorted into a dumpy room: a conference table, a whiteboard on one wall and, on the opposite wall, what must be a huge two-way mirror. It was right out of your basic TV crime drama.

Elliot and another guy, an analyst, soon came in. I give them the story again and then diagram out all the steps of the fraud as I know it on the whiteboard. Elliot and the other guy are taking pictures of the whiteboard with their iPhones.

After answering all their questions, Elliot and the analyst begin discussing jurisdictional issues. How can the Boston office get this case?

Nothing is resolved. They tell me I can go. They will get back to me. When I walk out to my car, I'm pretty pissed. But I also know I'm well past the point of being able to do nothing.

I was in. All in.

For the record, I never heard from the Boston FBI agents again.

CHAPTER 35

Bo Dietl & Associates

I left the Boston FBI office and drove straight to New London, CT to catch the ferry over to Long Island. I was pretty steamed the whole drive.

But after a half-hour or so, I realized I wasn't upset with the FBI. I understand the issue of jurisdiction. If they don't have jurisdiction, then they can't act. It's simple. I was actually kicking myself for not thinking about that ahead of time. I was mad at myself for not knowing.

I find being uncertain exhausting. I hate it. It can produce weapons-grade anxiety. Although I'm more used to uncertainty now, I still hate it. But the best way for me to combat anxiety is to accept the reality of the situation. Then I need to define a logical path forward.

So my thought process immediately goes to: How do I move this ball forward? What can trip me up? If I don't see a clear path out of this mess—and it is a mess—what do I need to learn to help me find that clear path?

To do that, I needed to know a few things.

First, who actually owned the vineyard? Southport claimed it owned 93 percent of the voting stock. But since August of last year, nine months earlier, the insurance company that provided the funds to buy it was under the control of the Delaware Insurance Commissioner.

Southport itself had put up no money. Yet it claimed—in writing—"undisputed ownership" of 93 percent of the capital stock in PBEV, worth at least $6 million in asset value.

We tried to contact the representatives for the Insurance Commissioner. Our lawyer called them. Sent them e-mails. He even sent letters via snail mail. But they never responded. Not once.

So, who owned this company?

Second, I needed to know if law enforcement was investigating this case. The FBI office in Boston now knew about it. But they were struggling with how to get jurisdiction. So I assumed the FBI was not on Southport's trail.

I also found it difficult to believe that I was the first and only one to contact law enforcement. The initial draft of the Duff & Phelps report had been circulating for over a year. That thing was pretty definitive. You don't need to be a criminal defense lawyer or prosecutor to read that and not think... something's not right here.

The Wall Street Journal had also published a follow-up article to the original. The second article examined Southport's claim to a painting by Caravaggio, the Baroque-era Italian artist. It seems Southport had made a down payment of $1.5 million in cash (remember S.I.D.?) to its owner. They also agreed to pay $38.5 million at a later date.

Then, in a fit of—brazenness? stupidity?—they put it on the books of Freestone Insurance for... wait for it... $128 million.

Not only did *The Wall Street Journal* question the value of the painting. It also questioned its authenticity! So, how could law enforcement not be investigating?

As I sat on the ferry making its way across Long Island Sound, I wrote down four questions:

1. How can I find out who owns the vineyard?
2. How do I find out if law enforcement is investigating?
3. If there's an investigation, who's conducting it?
4. How do I get in touch with them?

***

This was not my first brush with fraud and investigation during my time at the vineyard. One day an investigator for a large import-export company showed up at Premium Wine Group. It was early in my tenure at the vineyard when I got the heads-up call from Russell, the winemaker.

The investigator was asking when Premium was going to pay the amount owed to the importer. Russell informed him that we didn't owe any money to the importer. Not only that, but he had never even done business with them.

The next day, I sat down with Russell and reviewed the documents the investigator had left behind.

It seems a small wine company in New York had imported several thousand gallons of wine from France. Once it arrived in New York, he shipped it to Russell at Premium Wine Group. There, Russell's crew had, as contracted, put the wine into kegs. Once done, the small company picked it up and paid their bill.

The problem? The little company had somehow gotten Premium Wine Group's import license number. Why? Because the little company did not have one. Without such a license, you can't even get the wine onto the boat in France. Never mind bringing it into the United States.

To complicate matters, the guy not only didn't have a liquor license, but never paid the French vineyard from which he bought the wine. Then, the guy sold his wine all over Long Island at a below-market price and stiffed his vendors.

As a result, the vineyard in France and the shipper were looking to Premium Wine Group for their money.

The ripple effect for Premium Wine Group here was huge. If the New York State Liquor Authority, a notoriously difficult regulatory agency to deal with, believed Premium was complicit, that could mean a loss or suspension of its license.

Premium Wine Group made the wine for 17 or 18 brands on Long Island in 2014. The demand for rosé wine from Long Island wineries was now hitting stratospheric levels.

If Premium had to suspend operations, it would take down some big-name producers with it, not to mention Lieb Cellars and PBEV.

***

I wasn't quite sure what to do. So I called my friend, Joe Coffey.

I'd known Joe since the early 2000s, when I was working for an investment banking firm on Madison Avenue.

Jeff had introduced us at lunch somewhere in lower mid-town. That lunch turned into an afternoon, and one of the funniest I ever had. Joe is a lawyer and investor. He played football in high school and college. He was Irish Catholic. And his father was an NYPD detective—a very famous NYPD detective. Think Son of Sam and John Gotti.

We hit it off beautifully. Joe is a no-nonsense, no BS, no excuses fellow. It's awfully tough not to like him.

Because I was dealing with my little French wine importer problem, I knew I needed advice. So I called him.

I needed to learn all I could about this sneaky little Frenchman. In my mind, I was prepping for lawsuits, regulatory hearings, and lots of scrutiny. All this involving Premium Wine Group—a company I was still learning about.

I called Joe. He listened. Asked a few questions in a very lawyer-like way, and then said, "Send an e-mail to Bo Dietl. Use my name. Tell him you're my friend."

Not five minutes after I sent the e-mail to Bo, my phone rang. "I'm looking for Richard Bailey. This is Bo Dietl. Any friend of Joe Coffey is a friend of mine. How can we help you?"

Bo Dietl, among lots of other things, is a famous former NYPD detective. After leaving the NYPD, he started Bo Dietl & Associates, a private detective agency. He's also an actor and had a movie made about him.

I actually remembered him from his regular appearances on the "Imus in the Morning" radio show. My brother Tom and I were religious Imus listeners going all the way back to the early-mid 1970s, when we were doing stone mason work on the Thimble Islands, off the coast of our hometown of Branford, Connecticut.

In fact, we nicknamed our maternal grandmother after one of Imus' characters. A fine, dignified widow of a senior Goldman Sachs executive was known as "Granny Nuggerman" or just "Nuggerman" for nearly 20 years thanks to Imus.

Anyway, Bo's office is at One Penn Plaza, high above Madison Square Garden. As I was sitting in their conference room enjoying the killer view, Mike Ciravolo walked in. Bo is the firm's Chairman and CEO. Mike's the President.

Now, Mike is one of those guys who exudes a quiet, tough, "I've seen it all" confidence. When you find out he's a former NYPD cop, you have not one whit of surprise.

After explaining the situation, Mike outlines a plan. He's going to send a guy—a former detective from mid-town north—out to see me and we'll figure it out.

Within a day or two, I get a knock on the door of the Lieb Estate house, which is now my office. Now this guy looks like a TV detective, even down to the trench coat. We sit down, talk it out, and he says, "Okay, let me see what I can do."

Suffice it to say he solved the problem. Quickly. He prepared a report which we handed to the investigator for the import company. He thanked us. We never heard from him again.

But one final note on that: Our investigator showed up at the French guy's house. Ironically, it was only a few miles from the vineyard. He knocked on the door and asked his wife if he could speak with him. He wasn't home, she replied. Our guy left his card. We learned later that he suddenly returned to France.

***

So, the only way I can think of to get the Southport information to law enforcement and make them focus on it is to call Mike Ciravolo at Bo Dietl & Associates.

Talking to Mike Ciravolo on the phone is always like talking to someone you've known all your life. Like talking to your closest friend. Or your big brother. He asks about my wife, my kids, how I'm doing, etc. He's amazingly adept at putting you at ease.

He must have been one hell of an interrogator.

But then he gets down to business. And when that happens, he's all business.

By now, I have a verbal executive summary of this problem well-rehearsed. So, I give it to Mike. He asks a few questions and then says, "Why don't you come in and meet with us? I'll talk to Bo. We'll assemble a team to help you."

A team. Not really what I wanted to hear. See, I'm still kind of hoping I could hand this off to someone who would take it to law enforcement.

I want somebody else to do the dirty work.

But Bo and Mike's team dug hard and quickly produced a report.

Its first paragraph read, "In the course of trying to confirm the majority shareholders in a company managed by a client, we identified a blatant and obvious plundering of the assets of several insurance companies… It cries out for a criminal investigation."

They also produced the best outline of all the Southport companies I'd ever seen.

The ownership of the vineyard remained uncertain (there's that word again.) That meant I could tie the ownership question up in court for years.

Nice. I liked that.

Finally, when it came down to the subject of whether law enforcement was involved… they couldn't get any confirmation whatsoever. It was mystifying for everyone.

Bo, Mike, and their guys have lines of communication into all sorts of law enforcement agencies—not just New York City's but also state and federal.

In fact, one of their guys called a contact at the U.S. Attorney for the Southern District of Manhattan (SDNY) to try and refer it in. To his and everyone else's astonishment, he was waved off.

While sitting with Bo, Mike, and another one of their guys in Mike's office, they concluded that if the investigation isn't being run out of the SDNY, then the only thing that makes sense is that it's being run out of Washington. Out of main Justice.

"If so," I asked, "how do we get in touch with whoever's in charge of this thing there?"

Let us think about it, they said. We'll find a way.

Boy did they ever.

CHAPTER 36

A day or two later, I received a phone call from Mike Ciravolo. "Richard, we found someone who can help you," he said.

Mike explained that these guys are "top-notch" and have a strong white-collar practice. They're former prosecutors and former Assistant United States Attorneys (AUSA). They know how the U.S. Department of Justice works.

Mike made it clear to me that, in his professional opinion, this was a federal criminal case. There was too much money involved. Too many jurisdictions. To top it all off, the victims were insurance companies and their insureds—a huge complicating factor—could make things very messy.

There was no doubt in Mike's mind. This was a federal case. A big one too. In our last meeting in his office, he looked at me and said, "It's likely you're going to find yourself on the witness stand. You can't do this alone. You need a good lawyer."

"I gave them your contact information," he said. "They're going to call you."

Later that afternoon, while in bumper-to-bumper traffic on the Long Island Expressway, my phone rang. It was a 212 area code.

212 means an office in Manhattan. It wasn't Southport's number. It wasn't Bo Dietl's office. Those numbers I recognized. I had lots of Manhattan area code numbers in my phone that I recognized.

But this one? Never seen it before.

I'd already developed the habit of letting incoming calls I don't recognize go into voicemail. The Southport and vineyard situations were getting crazier by the week. A call from an unknown 212 area code had a very high likelihood of being bad news. At least so I thought. But I answered it anyway.

A very polite gentleman identified himself as an attorney with Cole Schotz, a law firm in New York. Bo Dietl & Associates had given him my phone number. He asked how he could help.

That was a pleasant surprise.

He asked a lot of questions, and I was pretty guarded in my responses. He was not my attorney yet. This was the first conversation.

Before I could hire his firm, he had to run an internal conflict of interest check. Law firms do that to make sure they don't already represent someone who may do business with you or may be after you for something.

But with Southport? Who knew? From all appearances, they had so much going on. I bet there were dozens of New York law firms who did business with Burns, Scherr, and the Southport Lane Boys' Club.

Now, I've been dealing with law firms and lawyers my entire career. I've had conflict checks come back where my selections were disqualified. So, I remained vague on the details I already knew.

Around that time, I was also starting to get a little paranoid. After all, my bosses *may* have committed federal crimes. I'm now having secret meetings with private detectives and have twice met with the FBI. I'd also guaranteed a $2 million bank loan for a company that was still losing money.

There was a whole lot going on. Not much of it was positive.

I didn't know who I could talk to about any of this shit. Here's the thing: You want to tell people about all the crazy stuff going on. But then you realize that knowing about the crazy stuff may drive them away. You need those people. So, you don't tell anyone.

Paranoia and anxiety now came in waves. One day I'd be on top of it. Another day I'd be under it.

But the conflict check came back clean. I was able to retain Cole Schotz to represent Premium Beverage Group Inc (PBEV).

***

Enter Michael Weinstein.

When something involves the government, I have this thing. I want to hire a lawyer who's worked there. I want one who has worked as close to the department I have to deal with as I can get.

I don't want Harvard or Yale theorists. Let them do the appellate and Supreme Court work. I sat in a conference room once when a high-minded Harvard theorist pissed off opposing counsel.

It didn't end well for us. Their Fordham-educated lawyer stuck it to us every chance he got.

This time I wanted someone who knew the DOJ inside and out. Someone who knew how a criminal case moves through the system. Someone who understood why the government agency makes decisions certain ways. I also wanted someone who knows how they came to that decision. What each step in the process looks like.

If they still have contacts inside the government, even better. Maybe that would get us a back-channel. The government loves back-channels.

Michael Weinstein had all that.

Right out of law school, he worked as a trial attorney at the Department of Justice in Washington, DC. Then he spent a few years as an Assistant United States Attorney for the District of Columbia.

That meant Michael had made prosecutorial decisions similar to the ones I wanted to insulate the vineyard from. He was smart, thoughtful, and smooth. Even better, underneath that polished exterior was someone who could play hardball.

Over the course of the next week to ten days, we spoke often. Michael also made a trip to the vineyard to get a look at the place.

It didn't take Michael long to make an impact.

***

Thursday June 11, 2015
Orient Point Ferry, Orient Point, NY

I'm sitting in my car waiting to board the ferry for the ride to New London when my phone rings. It's Weinstein. Now, Michael is a smooth, restrained lawyer type. So I'm caught off guard by the high excitement in his voice. He doesn't say hello. He just starts talking. The words are tumbling out of his mouth.

"Are you sitting down?" (I was behind the wheel of my car). "A huge task force is investigating Southport Lane. It's being run out of the Justice Department in Washington, DC. The FBI, SEC, and

DOJ are all involved. The lead investigator is an FBI agent out of Knoxville, Tennessee. I've spoken with him several times, including just now. He wants to meet you and would love to have your help. But the really big thing is, he wants to know if you'll wear a wire. If the answer is yes, they want to meet ASAP. This is big, Richard. This is really big."

A lot was running through my head. My first thought was that Bo Dietl and Mike Ciravolo were spot-on correct. This was being run out of Washington. That explained why the U.S. Attorney for the Southern District of New York passed on this.

The fact that there was a task force assigned to it was intimidating. And asking me to wear a wire? That I'd never thought about.

Finally, I also knew I had to tell my wife Christina, and that was not a conversation I looked forward to. I love her dearly. But she didn't sign up for this.

I asked Michael if I could think it through over the course of the weekend. He assured me that would be fine. We agreed to talk again on Monday.

Christina's reaction was classic … and cautionary. "I hope you know what you're doing." I didn't. It was also fatalistic. "I can tell you've already made up your mind to do this." I had. "So please be careful."

There it was. I was now all in.

***

When I'm all in, something happens with me. Personal consequences are no longer a factor. I'd had several life-threatening experiences in my life. To be quite frank, I found them all exhilarating. That kind of exhilaration is a drug. An incredible "gotta do it again" kind of drug.

But Chris didn't sign up for this. When I told her about one particular experience in my past, she didn't believe me. She thought I was making it up. I wasn't. But it really doesn't matter. I loved her and I had to tell her what I was going to do.

The following Monday, I told Michael Weinstein that I was in and to go ahead and set up the meeting.

Several hours later, he called me back. The meeting was set for Tuesday, June 23rd, 1:00 pm at his office on Third Ave. in Manhattan. He suggested I get there about 12:30 so we could prepare.

I agreed. Then I went back to trying to run the vineyard. But to be honest… my focus was solely on this next meeting with the FBI.

***

Tuesday June 23

As requested, I showed up at Michael's office on Third Ave. a half-hour before our meeting with the FBI. Good thing too. I was incredibly nervous. And when I get nervous, I perspire. Then I get embarrassed that I'm perspiring. That makes me more embarrassed, which makes me perspire more.

From 12:30 to 1:00 pm, I bet Michael handed me four or five glasses of ice water. It did the trick. I stopped perspiring. Somehow, I suspect I wasn't his first client to get the flop sweats before a meeting with the FBI. Probably won't be the last either. But he did calm me down. He also told me to follow his lead and answer their questions directly and honestly.

Most important, Michael reminded me that I was not in trouble. I was here to help *them*.

At exactly 1:00 pm, three federal agents arrived at Cole Schotz. It's like they waited outside for the clock to strike one. Peter and Joanne were from the Knoxville, Tennessee FBI field office. The third agent, Donald, was with the IRS Criminal Investigative Division.

Peter sat across the conference room table from me. He was about 35 to 40 and had one of the deepest southern accents I'd ever heard. He looked at me, smiled, and said, "Well, we might as well make this official." With that, all three pulled out what looked like small hardcover books and opened them. On one side was their badge, on the other their identification.

Peter was clearly in charge. I figured he must be a lawyer who'd once been in the army. He had a green notepad cover that said, "Judge Advocate General." He opened it and handed a document to Michael Weinstein. Michael looked it over and nodded back to Peter. I immediately suspected they had prepared for this moment.

Over the course of the next two hours, Peter asked questions, and I answered them. As I'd done in Boston, I provided the agents with copies of my excel spreadsheets. I also had copies of the Premium Wine Acquisition bank statements.

After more than two hours, Peter and the agents excused themselves from the conference room. During that time, Michael showed me the document Peter had handed him.

It was on the stationery of the U.S. Attorney for the Eastern District of Tennessee. It was a "proffer letter." What's worse, it listed me as a "defendant."

Now, a proffer is a written agreement between a prosecutor and a defendant or prospective witness. It's also known as a "Queen for a Day" letter." The agreement allows the defendant or witness to give the prosecutor information about an alleged crime. But it also limits the prosecutor's ability to use that information against him.

I looked at Michael, pointed to where it said "defendant," and said, "I'm not signing that. I'm not a defendant."

Michael looked at me and then pointed to the address on the letter. It was addressed to Michael at his office in New Jersey. Except it didn't say, "New Jersey." It said "Jew Jersey."

I never even noticed that. Michael rolled his eyes and said, "Gotta love the government." I didn't know what to do. But I did break up laughing.

***

A few moments later, the agents came back into the room. Michael called their attention to my objections to the letter.

"Yeah, we don't need that anymore," Peter said.

I immediately slid it into my backpack. I still have it.

Peter then began his sales pitch. He stated that this was not a victimless crime. There were thousands of individual victims in dozens of states. After years of paying their insurance bills, these folks woke up one day and had no insurance, all because of what Southport did.

Peter then looked directly at me and said, "Richard, are you willing to help us as a source in this investigation?"

I answered yes.

"Are you willing to wear a wire?"

I took a deep breath and answered, "Yes sir." Then I added, "I've seen a lot of fraud in my career. I've also been a victim of it. In one deal I did, the seller gave us fraudulent financial statements. I want the system to work. Plain and simple."

The next question bothered me for quite some time. Peter asked, "People may think you're a snitch. You okay with that?"

My response was simple and a bit defiant. "I'm not a snitch," I said. "I haven't committed any crime."

That was it. I was now a government asset in a criminal investigation. My life would never be the same.

***

A few minutes later, they gave me my code name.

"Since you make wine, we've given you the codename 'Brewer,'" Peter said, as if it was a clever play on my occupation. Frankly, I felt relieved. I even said "Brewer" was better than "Flounder," the code name Kent Dorfman had in the movie "Animal House."

No one laughed except me. I guess they were all too young.

Joanne then asked me for my phone. "I'm entering all our numbers. If you need us, call or text us. We'll get right back to you."

Then they taught me how to record calls using my phone. It's insanely easy. We even tried a few practice calls.

Simply put, there's no way to detect when or if your call is being recorded. It's pretty slick.

Then they asked me if I had any questions. I did. And it was an insanely stupid one. "Do they actually shave your chest hair when you wear a wire?" I asked, sounding like a befuddled teenager.

The entire room cracked up laughing. Looking around and quickly realizing the idiocy of my question, I broke up too.

"It's not like TV, Richard," Peter said in his deep Mississippi drawl.

For the first time, they then read me what they call my "Admonishments." This is essentially a long list of things I can't say or do. For example, I can't say I work for the government or the FBI. I cannot make promises or commitments on behalf of the government. Finally, if I get paid any money, I have to pay taxes on it.

Finally, they slid a piece of paper over to me. It was a copy of the admonishments they just had read to me.

I had to sign it. But I couldn't use my name. I had to sign it as "Brewer."

That done, Peter took the document and quickly placed it in his Army- green Judge Advocate General clipboard folder. We never got a copy.

Shortly after that, the meeting ended. All three agents thanked me. Peter said he'd be in touch shortly. Then they left. It was nearly 4:00 pm. I looked at Michael Weinstein and said, "I need a drink."

I walked over to my favorite little haunt, Palm Too on 2nd and 45th, and ordered a proper martini. Because I was staying the night at the Hilton a few blocks away, I had another. And another after that. Maybe even another after that as well. I'm not quite sure.

I actually don't remember if I ate either. I don't think I did… unless you consider the green olives in the martini as a vegetable.

Before that day, I'd never drunk for the express purpose of getting numb.

But this day was different.

CHAPTER 37

Some people have bursts of clear thinking when in the shower. I call those "shower epiphanies." Others are able to concentrate on something that bothers them when driving in the car. I do both.

When our two sons were growing up, I learned so much about them—and what was going on with them—when driving them in the car. It was like there was something freeing to them when we were alone in the car. Listening to their thought process, I came to understand them better and better.

What we learned in the car—and other places—allowed Chris and me to know that the boys were going to be fine on their own in this world. We taught them how to make good decisions. That's a parent's highest responsibility.

Anyway, for me, driving allows me time to focus on one problem at a time. I can't explain it. But I can separate the intellectual wheat from the chaff pretty quickly when I'm behind the wheel. I guess I hyper-focus.

***

After my "dinner" at Palm Too, I walked the three blocks back to my hotel. I took off my suit coat and tie and laid down on the bed. I woke up at 5:00 am the next morning, still in my suit pants and formerly starched shirt.

At 5:30 am, showered, shaved, and dressed (jeans and a gray t-shirt), I got into my car, headed to the Mid-Town Tunnel, and hopped onto the Long Island Expressway (aka, the L.I.E.).

The L.I.E. holds a special place in life with me. Good and bad. During my vineyard experience, I examined a lot of problems while driving on it, almost all of them as I was driving out of Manhattan. I learned over the years that when I took my problems *into* Manhattan, very often I came *out* of Manhattan with new ones.

This day, I kept going over and over my meeting with the FBI. There was something off. Something that didn't square up.

Then it hit me.

During the course of the initial two-hour interview with the FBI, they barely mentioned Alex Burns' name. Yeah, they asked how I met him. They asked about the "Shit I Did" moment. We also covered many of my conversations with Alex leading up to his sudden departure. But they never went into deep detail about Alex. We kind of went through my time with Alex as if they were checking off a box.

But when we got to Andrew Scherr and Rob McGraw, it was a whole different story. They wanted to know everything.

I'd always been careful around Andrew. Ever since that first meeting way back in March 2013, I'd been cautious around him. Andrew was sphynx-like to me. Self-disciplined, controlled, prudent, and measured, he was the 180-degree opposite of Alex. He was very, very difficult for me to read. Over time, I learned that you had to weigh what Andrew said very carefully.

Alex Burns needed to impress and overwhelm everyone. Andrew Scherr never showed the slightest desire to do the same. He was a practitioner of soft power. And after Alex bugged out—18 months before—Andrew had all the power. Southport Lane, and whatever it was at the time, belonged entirely to him.

Slowly, over the course of the previous 18 months, it became clear: Andrew was trying to keep whatever he could salvage out of Southport all to himself. Southport's CFO once actually described Southport to me now as "Andrew's Empire."

It wasn't a realistic goal. But what at Southport was realistic? It was a fantasy land for journeymen financiers. It was a private equity firm for people with no experience in private equity.

Andrew never directly asserted his power, at least not with me. He didn't need to. He was too smooth for that. Instead, he'd always appeal calmly and with impeccable reason to my sense of logic. Smart move on his part.

I've always suspected that Andrew must have had a sky-high emotional intelligence. The ability to perceive, use, understand, manage, and handle emotions.

That also highlighted what I thought was his most worrisome characteristic —his cold-blooded, transactional approach to nearly everything, at least from what I saw.

But in appealing to my logic, he read me perfectly. Well… almost.

The FBI also wanted to know a lot more about Rob McGraw. When I brought up his name in that first meeting, I told them, "Rob is the real brains of this outfit. He's a structured finance guy, and no one is better at creating a house of cards than a structured finance guy."

And make no mistake, Southport was a house of cards.

In the late 1980s, I took a New York Institute of Finance course on structured finance. It was all the rage. Almost one-third of all savings and loan companies in the United States were failing then.

Jimmy Carter deregulated savings and loan institutions in 1980. For the next 10 to 15 years, these small, loosely regulated institutions loaded up on all sorts of high-risk assets. Then one day, as they must, the chickens came home to roost. The high-risk assets went bad and took 1,043 of the country's 3,234 savings and loans down with them.

Structured finance aimed to solve that problem. How? Simple. Set up a new corporation—known as a collateralized debt obligation (CDO)—to own the risky assets instead of the bank. Oh… and the higher the risk, the higher the fees for the underwriters who sold the CDO shares to investors, and for the bank-sponsor doing the loan underwriting. So, by transferring the risk of default from the bank to the CDO, the bank or S&L found itself in the perfect position.

The new money raised by the CDO allowed them to make more loans. The riskier the loan, the higher the fees and the rates. So guess what… the S&Ls made risker loans! The investors were also the beneficiaries of these higher interest rates. But for that, the investor also owned 100 percent of the risk for failure. But not the S&L!

High fees with no risk? Brilliant! Unless you invested in the CDO.

In about 1990, I wanted to set up a company that would buy accounts receivables in the steel industry where I worked at the time. Our company was a classic 1980s style Leveraged Buy Out (LBO). The company was worth $6 million. They paid $8 million for it, then borrowed about $10 million. In 1990, they were in bankruptcy.

I wanted to set up a structured finance company that would buy accounts receivables. In the steel industry back then, the cash-to-cash cycle was extremely long. It could easily run five to six months from the time you paid your vendors to the time you collected from your customers.

If I could bridge that gap, they could pay me a fee or we could buy the accounts receivable at a discount. Either way, it sounded like fun and the numbers were enormous from our customers alone. I even had interest from Credit Suisse First Boston in putting it together. We did do a version of it back then with Japanese global trading giant Mitsui & Co. So I knew it worked. But it never came to pass. My timing was off. By about 10 years.

***

Rob McGraw is a quiet, shy young guy. He's polite. He's also whip-smart. You could see that early on in any conversation you had with him.

But he could—and I always attributed this to either his shyness or his shitty people skills—come off as an arrogant son of a bitch as well. One time, when we were talking about Southport's precarious position, he said, "Yeah, I don't really care about this place. My wife has a good job."

Wowww! That's fucking cold.

But the speed with which his thought process worked was also impressive. I found that you could ask him almost anything. He would go quiet for a moment, then respond with a well-articulated and fully considered opinion. I admired that.

I liked him too. In an office full of journeymen want-to-be financiers, Rob stood out as a thinker. Everyone else was either a salesman, a bookkeeper, or a lawyer. Rob was different.

After my first few meetings with him, I asked Alex Burns if I could run things by Rob on occasion and work with him. Oddly, Alex vehemently responded, "NO!"

Rob had a bachelor's and an MBA from New York University. He had worked at a big accounting company's tax department. Then he went on to Merrill Lynch, where he worked in the Fixed Income Capital Markets group.

When he became bored with big firm life, Alex Burns recruited him to Southport Lane. Alex was trying to securitize "non-tradi-tional assets." Then he wanted to sell them to insurance companies. Seeing an intellectual challenge, Rob left Merrill Lynch and joined Southport Lane.

For a smart, ambitious young guy, it must have been viewed as a risky move that also had the possibility of being enormously lucrative. A potential Master of the Universe type pay-off.

But in reality… it would be the biggest mistake of his life. Which is a shame too. We disagreed on a lot. But he was a decent guy.

***

From December 2013 on, Rob and I clashed over the resolu-tion of the Preferred Stock of PBEV. It had been nearly two years since I'd signed the certificates. U.S. Bank, the fifth largest commer-cial bank in North America, served as the custodian of Southport's assets.

Now, those preferred shares were on U.S. Bank's books for $10 million. Remember, when I issued them, they were worth only $1.2 million. How they got up to $10 million remains a mystery to me.

In one phone call a few months earlier, it all came to a head. Rob became very angry with me. He said I have no say in the mat-ter, that my function was "purely ministerial."

When I countered and asked how did $1.2 million become $10 million, he responded that it was "not my concern."

My reaction was quick and angry. "It is my concern because my signature is on those certificates."

Hugh Hill then made what I took to be a veiled threat about all the trouble I might find myself in if I didn't reissue them. He may not have meant it that way. But I took at as a threat.

My anger rose even more. "Are you saying I may have criminal liability on this?" There it was—the "c" word.

No one answered.

Andrew Scherr then piped in as the voice of reason. "No one is saying anything of the sort, Richard. If you're uncomfortable doing this, then we'll have to figure out another way."

Classic Andrew. Calming and reassuring. Then he slips in the veiled threat that "we'll have to figure out another way." He leaves unsaid that it may be at my peril.

I recounted this conversation to the FBI in Michael Weinstein's office. Making veiled and subtle threats that I may have criminal liability was a turning point for me.

I mean… another turning point. To be fair, there were lots of turning points.

But the guys at Southport were not acting like innocent men out to find the truth. Quite the opposite. They were acting like they had something to hide.

To me, Rob McGraw had protested too much. If this was all orchestrated by Alex, why is Rob, a quiet and mild-mannered guy, losing his shit over this? Why threaten me when I had no idea how this happened (I still don't).

Later on, Peter, the lead FBI agent, said to Michael Weinstein and me, "Do not reissue those preferred shares. That was definitely illegal." That's all I had to hear.

My goals at the time were simple:

1. To keep the vineyard open and running.
2. To keep Southport from getting involved in the vineyard. After all, we had cash in the bank from the loan I'd guaranteed. I also now knew Southport was being investigated for federal crimes. I worried that somehow, some way, they would try to seize that cash for themselves.
3. I also needed to learn as much as possible about what the hell happened.

The FBI's focus was on Scherr, McGraw, and a few others. The name Alex Burns rarely came up any more. So, following their lead, I began asking questions of the folks at Southport. Lots of them. Frankly, I'm surprised they never caught on. Maybe they did. Who knows? But I doubt it since they kept talking to me for another two years.

I also started sending the FBI, via my personal email account, boatloads of documents I'd collected over time, including a lot of e-mails. Some of the files were so large that they bounced back.

They were too big for the FBI servers. So, I set up a dedicated Dropbox account. The only two with access were me and Joanne, one of the agents who attended the meeting at Weinstein's office.

While all this was going on, lead agent Peter was calling with a lot of questions. I could only guess that they were doing some sort of background check of me to better know who they were dealing with.

I suppose I passed.

Also around this time, I started chatting regularly with Hugh, Southport's in-house counsel. I figured he was in a position to know all. Hugh hadn't been around when Burns, Scherr, and McGraw were concocting their schemes. But I figured, because he came in after that craziness, he might be willing to shed some light on just what the fuck had happened there.

One day in June 2015, on one of the first calls I taped, I was asking Hugh about Alex Burns. I was intentionally being a bit provocative. My thesis was that Alex, even though he was smart, lacked the knowledge and experience to orchestrate this fraud..

To me, what Southport had done was neither clever nor smart. Was it elaborate? Sure. Was it complex? Absolutely. But that was only because of the sheer number of intermediary companies they sold and resold, and the assets they had "purchased" from the insurance companies. Some of these assets passed through five or six shell companies. That part I'd already figured out.

How they thought that was clever is beyond me.

Passing assets through a series of intermediary companies provided no value except to separate those assets from the liability in the original transaction. It's just the corporate equivalent of the 1980s sidewalk hustle known as "Three Card Monti." It's simple sleight of hand. Also, it's easily traceable. How do I know? I did it.

I went on to theorize to Hugh that McGraw had to be involved. I even said that to Hugh, phrasing it this way: "McGraw had the smarts and brains Burns thought he had."

The answer was unforgettable.

"Yep," he said. "McGraw structured the deals, and Burns sold the lie."

Seconds after I got off the phone with Hugh, I texted the FBI. Bingo and confirmation. I had them.

CHAPTER 38

The events leading up to and including my meeting at Southport's offices on September 8, 2015 remain crystal clear to me.

Let me explain.

Since meeting the team of federal agents in June, lead agent Peter and I spoke often. Not only did he ask a lot of personal questions about me, but he asked a lot of questions about Southport personnel too. Do I know this person? Ever heard of this guy? What do you know about this person? What are they like?

Every time I spoke to Peter, I'd call Michael Weinstein to keep him in the loop.

The procedure for each of these calls was always the same. I'd get a text from Peter: "Have time for a quick call?"

"Sure," I'd always respond.

Because it was summer, my two sons were home from school. After texting Peter back, I'd excuse myself and go out to my car to take his call. Until my sons started asking simple, reasonable questions like, "Why do you go sit in the car in the driveway to talk on the phone? Who are you talking to?"

"Work shit," I'd grunt in return.

To my wife, who knew a little of what I was up to, I'd roll my eyes and whisper, "Government stuff."

So, I stopped sitting in the driveway. I found it easier to go for a ride.

There are five public beaches in my town. One has particularly good cell service. I wound up there a lot.

My calls with Peter were never long. That's one thing about working with the FBI. They ain't chatty. At least Peter wasn't. You get on the call, there was usually 15 to 20 seconds of niceties, then straight to the point.

Immediately after hanging up with Peter, I'd call Michael Weinstein. In those weeks, we spoke so often he had made it onto my iPhone's favorites screen. (He's still there.)

The FBI was keen to get a sense for what was going on at Southport. So, for a few weeks, I was in a version of the old-fashioned kids' game of "Telephone."

During this period, I rarely heard from Rob McGraw or Dean, the comptroller. If Andrew or Hugh called me, I'd let it go into voicemail. Then I'd immediately call them back. When that call was over, I'd text Peter informing him of the call. He would then call me back. After that call was over, I'd immediately call Weinstein to keep him in the loop and get his take on things.

It could get pretty rambunctious at times. There were days when that game of "Telephone" happened two, three, even four times in a single afternoon. I'd speak to someone at Southport, then to the FBI, and then to Weinstein so often that Michael exclaimed, "Look at you! You're at the center of a national case!"

He may have been right. I don't know. I'm not going to lie. It was deadly serious stuff, and once again my production of stress hormones was sky-high, as if I needed more stress in my life.

It also always seemed like these calls happened late in the afternoon. Almost as if I, or the vineyard, was the last thing on Southport's agenda. I probably was. After all, as we would later learn, the vineyard represented a minuscule part of Southport's problems.

When I was at the vineyard during the week, one of these call cycles began at almost 5:00 pm. After hanging around the vineyard house all day, quite often I needed to get out at night. I couldn't go to one of our tasting rooms for fear my calls would be overheard. So I started going to Greenport Harbor Brewing Company's new beer hall in nearby Peconic.

It was a fantastic open-air beer hall. They also had a killer food truck that made an awesome cheeseburger. Best of all, it was only about three miles from Lieb Vineyards.

Even better for me on late weekday afternoons, it wasn't very busy. I could sit down, enjoy the view, have a beer, make these telephone calls, and not be within 100 feet of other people.

The brewery was new then and if you ordered a pint of your favorite beer, they gave you the pint glass with their logo as a thank-you. Within a few months, I had a cabinet full of them. Still do!

***

It was also a very busy time at the vineyard. The late summer season was upon us, and the tasting rooms at Lieb Cellars were full.

This was the third Lieb summer for Ami Opisso. Mine, too. I now understood the rhythms of the business and how the cash flowed. I knew when we could spend and when we couldn't.

Ami now had the operational side humming. It had taken a lot of work, a lot of mistakes, and a lot of worry to get to this point. But we made it.

One time a year or so earlier, she'd broken into tears during a meeting, telling me she "had never failed at anything." Now, Ami is a tough cookie. She's super-smart, cerebral, supremely organized, and fantastic at assessing a problem and mapping out the steps to its solution. For her to get that upset meant her stress levels were off-the-chart as well.

I remember telling her, "You have not failed, and you are not going to fail. We took over a horrible mess. We will be successful, but success takes time." Ami gave everything she had to this turn-around. I'll be grateful forever. Without her, we would have died.

Lieb Cellars eventually did survive. But we weren't out of the woods yet.

Everyone in the company knew the vision. Everyone knew the mission. Everyone bought into both. Constant communication with those who report to you remains critical. That is how you find chinks in your armor.

Also, everyone knew their role, and most importantly, everyone knew how their performance affected their pay. My father, a commissioned stockbroker for 40 years, once said to me, "When you grab them by their W-2's, their hearts and minds will follow." Truer words were never spoken.

So, after a year or two of nail-biting, Ami and her crew were now beginning to reap the rewards. You could see the enthusiasm in their faces and hear it in their voices. That attitude is contagious, and success breeds success.

Or, as my high school football coach liked to say, the harder you work, the luckier you get. Ami and her crew were living proof of that.

Lieb Wines and our second label, Bridge Lane Wines, were getting traction. Not only in the retail markets but the wholesale markets as well. Lieb and Bridge Lane wines were now sold not only in New York but in six other states.

Before I left in 2018, we would be in 13 states, selling our wine in 750ml bottles, 20L kegs, 3L boxes, and 350ml cans. During that time, Lieb Cellars sales would go from 3,700 cases per year to over 30,000, almost an eight-fold increase. Ami and her team worked their tails off to get there. It was and is a remarkable achievement.

And I made sure it showed up in their pay!

***

If the end of the summer at Lieb Cellars is a full-on sprint, at Premium Wine Group it's the quiet before the storm. The 2015 harvest season would start soon. The industrial-sized winemaking facility was ready. Russell Hearn and his crew had been at this for 15 years. They knew exactly what they were doing.

The presses were clean and in place. The tanks were empty and cleaned. The entire 20,000 square-foot facility was ready.

Harvest is always a madhouse at Premium. Fruit from our customers comes in at all hours of the day and night. The presses often ran 20 hours a day.

We did not know this yet, but 2015 would turn out to be a record-setting harvest. Russell nicknamed it the "Tsunami Harvest." The fruit kept coming and coming from all our customers.

After all, it had been a spectacular growing season. Warm days and cool nights with low humidity—perfect for maximizing crop yields. That also meant it would be an outsized revenue and billing year for Premium. That made my life much easier.

Everything was moving forward according to plan.

Then Hugh Hill called.

Now, in the current situation, calls from Andrew and Hugh produced a quick and sudden stress spike in me. Call it an adrenaline surge. Call it a cortisol spike. It doesn't matter. I could be in a great mood, enjoying the day, basking in the sunshine, having fun outdoors with my wife, my sons, or both.

But the minute I saw it was Andrew or Hugh calling me, my first reaction was generally "shit!"

First, let me clarify. Hugh and I were always cordial and professional with each other. On occasion, he would drop the lawyerly visage, and we spoke candidly about the mess Southport was in. Hugh was very much aware a large-scale fraud had taken place at Southport. But I always thought his insistence it was 100 percent Alex Burns' fault was unrealistic. But what I think doesn't matter. Burns was guilty as hell of the crimes committed against the insurance companies.

My intent was to get Hugh to understand that I, too, knew a large-scale fraud had occurred without setting off any alarm bells. My overarching goal was simple. I wanted to isolate the vineyard from the mess of Southport.

Hugh had joined Southport in the fall of 2013, only a few months after me and before Burns said, "Oh fuck, oh fuck, oh fuck. I hate my insurance companies," and walked out. So, he played no part in Southport's problems. His goal was to clean it up. Like most of us, he had no idea what he was stepping into when he joined up.

But now, as Southport's General Counsel, he was in a tough spot. He represented the company, which means not only the shareholders but the investors, creditors, and employees.

There's this little trigger in business law once a company becomes "insolvent." Believe it or not, most managers don't know this. But I've worked on a lot of companies that were insolvent. As a result, I've come to know this trigger better than most non-lawyers.

If a company is unable to pay its debts in the ordinary course of business, then the managers must put the interests of its stakeholders ahead of shareholders. Therefore, the managers must act in the interests of the creditors. That means the banks, the secured lenders, the unsecured trade creditors, the equity holders—in this case, Southport Lane and Andrew Scherr as Southport's sole owner—go to the back of the line.

While I never saw Southport's financial statements, I had to believe they were insolvent. How could they not be? The core of their business rested on a crime.

So I suspected that Hugh, as General Counsel, was between a rock and a hard place. As Andrew moved and counter-moved, Hugh had no choice but to act in the best interests of and for the benefit of Southport's true creditors (the Freestone Estate, Blue-Cross BlueShield of South Carolina, and U.S. Bank, as well as the larger insurance regulatory community). I never saw him act directly or indirectly for Andrew's benefit, and I don't mean to suggest he committed any malfeasance. But I have no doubt he was in a very tight spot. There were a lot of eyeballs on Southport.

With most lawyers I know, I can tell within seconds if a phone call from them is going to be a good one or a bad one. It's in their tone, language, and mannerisms. It's the first thing I note. I listen for the formal tone, the lack of emotion, the "I'm delivering bad news" voice. As opposed to the "hey, let me give you an update" call, which often begins with some humorous chit-chat.

This call was all business. Hugh asked me to come into Southport's new offices the following week to "discuss the vineyard." When I asked him if anything particular was on the agenda, he replied tersely, "the future of the vineyard."

Oh shit, I thought.

My favorite FBI agent had a different reaction. He was clearly excited. Peter saw this as an ideal moment to get a glimpse of Southport's inner workings.

The meeting was set for 11:00 am on Tuesday, September 8th.

CHAPTER 39

In the days leading up to this meeting, I learned Southport had moved their offices to downtown Manhattan—17 South Street to be exact. The very bottom tip of Manhattan.

They had also changed their name. They were no longer Southport Lane. They were now called "Massive Holdings LLC."

I still get a kick out of this. *Massive Holdings? Of what?* Shitty assets bought with the proceeds of a white-collar crime wave? When I first heard of the name change, my reaction was a baffled, "Whaaaat?" With these guys, there was a strong element of "The Gang That Couldn't Shoot Straight."

What a stupid name. Alex Burns would have thought of something way more clever. And, had it been up to me, I'd have suggested "Sisyphus Holdings."

***

I was once again in contact with Peter several times each day. It was clear this meeting was a big deal to him. The plan was to meet in Manhattan two hours before I was to arrive at Southport (*sorry, Massive Holdings*). Peter and Donny, the IRS criminal investigator, would come to my hotel and brief me on what they needed me to do. I asked them where they were staying, thinking I'd make it easier for them, and received a vague response—Midtown, West Side.

I decided that I'd stay at a Hilton in the same general area. They were fine with that. It was clear they didn't want me staying in the same hotel as them.

Okay. Whatever.

The night before the meeting, I checked into a truly seedy Hilton Garden Inn in Times Square. To make matters worse, I pulled into and valet'd my car, only to go inside and find out I was at the wrong Hilton. I was about five blocks from where I was supposed to be.

Instead of getting my car, I decided to schlep my bags through the madness of Times Square. It didn't help that it was a hot and steamy night in late summer. Times Square, as usual, was pulsating with tourists. When I arrived at the right hotel, I was a sopping mess. The front desk crew must have looked at me and said, "Uh-oh."

Not a good start.

When I finally got to my room, I turned the air conditioning down to the temperature of a meat locker. An hour or so later, I ordered room service.

I never ate the meal.

Before dinner arrived, I found myself in the throes of a lengthy, first-class panic-anxiety attack. I hadn't had one in a couple of years.

If you've never had one, they're scary as hell. The first one I had was during the Labor Day weekend of 2001. It was a Sunday. My son Alex, then six years old, was sitting on my lap as I read to him.

Suddenly, I thought I was having a heart attack. I didn't have pain in my arms or my shoulders, but I felt that my heart was pounding out of my chest. I broke out in a cold sweat and felt a sense of impending doom.

I got Alex off my lap and asked him to get Mom. Alex then looked at me and said, "Is this what *deaf* looks like?" He had a slight lisp.

Christina came in, took a look at me, and asked Alex to run next door and get our neighbor Donna, who was a nurse. Well, Donna was working, so her husband John, who owned a paper-hanging business, came over instead.

He took one look at me and said, "I'm calling an ambulance."

It took about five minutes before the ambulance showed up. By then, all my symptoms had gone away. I felt fine. But they took me to the hospital anyway. I was released the next morning. I even went to the gym and got on the treadmill that same afternoon.

Weird.

Since then, I've always considered these lovely panic attacks a special hereditary gift from my father, who called them "the jim-jams." As in, "I had a case of the jim-jams."

But my dad went over on D-Day in a glider. He was just north of Bastogne during the Battle of the Bulge. And he secured the gas chamber at Dachau. He earned his.

Me? I'm not exactly risking my life here. But the jim-jams don't care.

I'm lying on the bed in a shitty hotel in Times Square. My heart is pounding through my chest. I have chest pains and an overwhelming fear I'm dying.

It goes on like this for several hours. As always, I consider dialing 911. But I know the symptoms. I know it's an anxiety attack, and I know it will pass. But this one's a doozy. It lasts far longer than any previous one

But when they're over, I drift into a deep, deep sleep. So, no dinner.

At 6:00 am, the jim-jams were long since over.

Like that first time in 2001, I decided to get some exercise. It's a way of saying "fuck you" to the panic attack. So, I went for a walk.

You see a very different side of Manhattan at 6:00 in the morning. The glitz and the glamor are gone. The flashing lights have dimmed. The streets are quiet. The only vehicles to be seen are trucks making deliveries or picking up last night's garbage. This is the Manhattan few tourists ever see. For some odd reason, it has always been one of my favorite parts of the day in New York. What can I say? I'm an infrastructure guy.

As is usually the case, the agents text me at 9:00 am sharp. I give them my room number. Moments later, there's a knock on the door. As Peter and Donnie enter the room, they step over my uneaten room service from last night. There's about 24 inches from the side of the bed to the walls. Peter looks around and remarks, "Jesus, Richard. What a dump! I feel like I'm doing a drug deal."

I told you it was a shitty hotel.

The two proceeded to brief me on the day's plan. They have specific questions they want me to ask. Don't be afraid to get argumentative or to pick a fight if necessary, they say. I took copious notes.

They also want me to make a map of Southport offices. Where are the file cabinets? Is there a computer closet? Whose office is whose? "Better yet, ask for a tour."

Finally, as soon as the Southport meeting ends, I'm to text them. They will instruct me where to meet.

Then they wired me up.

Now… let me get this over with. It's not a wire. It's not like anything you've seen on TV. There are no microphones poking out between the buttons of my shirt. Nothing under the lapel of my blue blazer. Nothing like that at all.

It could be anything. It could look like a pen with a special cap. It can look like a battery from an old Motorola flip phone or a medical device. It could look like a metallic commuter coffee mug, a tie clasp, or just about anything.

It doesn't even have to be exposed. It can be in my pocket, wallet, or backpack.

Peter handed me two devices. He told me to put one in the pocket of my favorite blue blazer—the one with my grandfather's 24 karat gold buttons. The other one should go in my shirt pocket—one of those boringly average Brooks Brothers button-down collared shirts I'd been wearing since college.

So, unless I slipped or fell or did something stupid, no one would ever see them. No one would ever know.

Then, suddenly, all conversation stopped. Both agents shook my hand and left.

I pick up my bags and head for the door.

I'm on my own. But then again, I'm not.

CHAPTER 40

Suddenly, being wired up didn't feel weird at all. In fact, I forgot all about it because when I hit the hotel door and was out on the street in the middle of the Times Square maw, which requires me to focus on where I am and where I'm going, I'm struck by one simple thing: It's an absolutely gorgeous day.

But I still must haul my bags the five blocks to the other Hilton where I'd valet'd my car. At least it isn't a muggy steamy mess like it was last night. *Be grateful for the little things*, the voice in my head is telling me. Not a cloud in the sky, 70 degrees, and all that awful humidity is gone.

So I'm grateful... for about three seconds.

In my own warped perspective, I'm now getting antsy because it's taking so long for the valet to bring my car around. I don't know why. It always takes about 30 minutes for a hotel valet to get your car in NYC. It's not like I haven't done this a couple of hundred times over the last 40 years.

Like most people, I have a lot of little personal tics. But when walking in New York City, one of mine is to regularly reach my right hand behind me and lightly tap my wallet to make sure I haven't lost it or been pickpocketed.

I don't know when or where I picked that one up—probably from hanging out in the city during the bad old days during the '70s or '80s. Thinking back, it sounds like something my father probably told me to do.

But today is a bit different. Not only do I tap my back pocket, but I also tap my blazer pocket and my shirt pocket while simultaneously checking my backpack for the camera disguised as a coffee mug. I want to make sure I haven't lost or dropped any of the new toys the government just gave me.

This causes my Reebok duffle bag to slip off my shoulder onto the sidewalk. I grab it. Pick it up, sling it back over my shoulder, and then I tap my back pocket, my blazer pocket, my shirt pocket, and the side pocket of my duffle bag.

Everything is still in place. But I glance at my watch. *Shit, I'm gonna be late.* I'm starting to get anxious again.

My normally threadbare patience is becoming a little thinner than usual this morning. I want my car. Now!

You see, I have to get all the way downtown, find a garage, park, and get to Southport's offices. I'm not very familiar with lower Manhattan. I have no idea what traffic is going to be like. Should I just bomb down Broadway the whole way? Should I cut over to the FDR Drive?

I have to be there in 45 minutes. No way am I going to be late. Punctuality is a sign of respect. A sign of good manners. To be on time is to be late. To be 10 minutes early is to be on time. To show up after the appointed time… well, that's plain bad manners. A sign you didn't think ahead. If you know you're going to be late, at least call ahead.

Or in today's world, text ahead. I know being 10 to 15 minutes late in Manhattan is no big deal. Except to me.

When my car finally shows up 20 minutes later, my suit coat is off, and I sling my bags in the back in a matter of seconds. I tip the driver and hop behind the wheel.

But before I pull out into the street, first things first, I put the air conditioning on so high you could make ice cream. I don't care. At least I won't be a nervous, sweaty mess. Nervous? Well, yeah probably. But sweaty? Nope.

Oh, and I text my favorite FBI agent and then separately Andrew Scherr to tell them I'm going to be a few minutes late. Never underestimate the power of good manners!

***

Now, there is something almost surreal about wearing a wire. You become profoundly aware of every syllable you utter. You're all alone. But you know you're not.

Your thought process—at least mine—flicks into overdrive as you calibrate everything you say against the backdrop of what the FBI will think about it.

I'm not worried about sounding stupid. I'm sure people react that way to me all the time. But I don't want to be flippant either. I also tend to think out loud. To talk to myself. Even argue with myself.

Frequently, I'll sit at home—or anywhere actually—in a lengthy silence, working something out in my head. My wife will ask, "Who you arguing with over there?"

She knows me. She knows I have to mentally work through every imaginable facet of an argument. It's how my brain works.

But I better not have an argument with myself out loud while wearing a wire. The FBI may think I'm crazy. I'm not.

***

After getting across town to the FDR Drive, I luck out. Traffic is moving very well. Still, I'm trying not to talk to myself or to curse at each and every indignity Manhattan traffic constantly throws at you.

I remind myself: Someone is listening!

Southport's new offices are at 17 South Street in lower Manhattan. Southport-Massive is subleasing office space from a family office called The Abernathy Group, whoever they are. I don't care. It doesn't matter.

I pulled into a parking garage on Broad Street. It was exactly across the street from Southport's office building. I handed the attendant the keys, told him I'd be less than two hours, grabbed my suit coat and backpack, and I was off.

My phone was in my hand when I felt it vibrate from an incoming text message. It was Peter, who simply said, "In place. See you."

Now that's kind of jolting. So, I guess that also means they saw me stop dead in the middle of Broad Street and look around. Where the hell were they? I had no idea. I was also lucky I didn't get hit by a bus.

Stopping in the middle of a busy Manhattan street is such an amateur move. So, I kept walking. But I was still looking around. Where were they?

As I walked into the building, something really weird happened. Time seemed to slow down. My eyes were wide open. I felt like my peripheral vision widened. I became calm as can be.

No nerves. No flop sweats. Nothing. Total focus.

Luckily, I rode up in the elevator alone. When I reached the 17th floor, I looked in the mirror and openly imitated Roy Scheider from "All That Jazz." Primarily for Peter's benefit—but partially for mine—I smiled and said, "Showtime."

I knocked on the door of Abernathy & Co as directed. Nothing. So I knocked again. Nothing again. Then, a few moments later, a door opened about 20 yards to my right. Andrew Scherr poked his head out.

Hmm… I knocked on the front office door, and someone came out an unmarked door 20 yards away. I made an instant mental note on that one for the FBI.

Andrew said, "Wait right there," popped back into the office, and closed that door. Within a few seconds, he opened the front office door where I was standing. As always, Andrew Scherr was the picture of politeness.

We walked into a small reception area. It looked old, almost like a Victorian parlor room. Or, as is so often the case on Wall Street, it's set up to look that way.

We took a right through a small door and were in Southport-Massive's conference room. It was not pretty. It was functional. A conference table, some filing cabinets, some bookshelves. Nothing remarkable.

"Nice place!" I said. "How about a quick tour?"

Inside of a minute later, I'm back at the conference table. Not much to see on the tour. Only a few offices. This was not Class AAA executive office space. It reminded me more of the back office of a brokerage firm. Purely functional. Nothing remarkable.

But at least I had a mental picture of the office layout, including the file cabinet locations. Not exactly a Kreskin-esque feat of mnemonics, though. Everything was straightforward and in plain sight.

The meeting itself was by turns contentious and mundane. Southport-Massive wanted to put the vineyard up for sale. Of course, they did. And who would get the money? They would and I'd be out of a job.

There was only one problem: They didn't own the vineyard any more. If they decided to assert their ownership, I knew I could tie them up in court for at least a year.

But again, today was not the day to play that card.

So, while they wanted me to hire a real estate agent, I argued that we needed to find an Merger & Acquisition broker. There was a lot of back and forth on this issue.

I was trying, rather forcefully, to impress upon them that if this was to go forward, I needed to handle the process. The reason? Well, I argued, if we put a for-sale sign out on the lawn, our business would dry up. Wholesalers would stop devoting resources to marketing our products.

But the wholesalers weren't really investing in us. That's not the way wholesale wine distribution works. We invest more in them than they ever invest in us. But Southport didn't know that, and so that argument seemed to stick.

Kind of out of the blue, I changed the subject. Looking around, I said, "Wait… At the old office, one whole wall was lined with filing cabinets. Where'd all those old files go?"

"They're all in a warehouse in New Jersey," someone answered.

"What about the painting—the Caravaggio they mentioned in *The Wall Street Journal*?" I asked.

"Warehouse," Andrew replied tersely. I sensed a little frustration in his voice. I also thought it would provoke immediate suspicion if I asked, "What warehouse? Where?" So, I let it go.

It was around 12:30, and someone brought up lunch. I politely declined even though I was starving. After all, I hadn't eaten dinner the previous night, though I did grab a bagel during my morning walk around Times Square.

But as usual, I wanted to get through the Mid-Town Tunnel and onto the L.I.E. by 1:00 pm. It was going to be tight. Also, I had no idea what Peter had in store for me after this meeting was over.

As we were wrapping up, Andrew Scherr said, "Hold on. We'll ride down with you."

Here it comes. I knew it. Suddenly, I'm having fun.

I hopped in the elevator with Andrew, Hugh Hill, and Rob Mc-Graw. I was backed into the corner when I remembered to text

Peter. Everyone is in front of me, so I can pull my phone out and type without anyone looking over my shoulder.

It's a simple message. "Coming Out. Not alone."

Rob McGraw cracked a joke: "You know, Richard, you'll probably get your picture taken and be sued just for being seen with us."

I break into a big smile as I hit the send button for the terse text to Peter. I quip to Rob, "I'll do the jokes, thanks." Everyone in the elevator laughed.

If he only knew. The irony was awesome.

We walked out the door to what was still a beautiful day. Outside the plaza in front of the building, Andrew pulled me aside for a brief private chat. Hugh and Rob walked off in search of lunch.

At precisely that moment, as Andrew and I were separating ourselves from the crowd for a little privacy, I spotted them.

Peter and Donnie were less than 50 yards away. And Donnie was pointing a big-ass camera directly at us.

Trying not to appear distracted, I realize that Donny's camera angle will only get the back of Andrew's head. So, feigning that the sun was in my eyes, I took two steps to my right. Andrew mirrored me and took two steps to his right.

The IRS criminal investigation agent now has a perfect headshot of Andrew.

That's when Andrew Scherr leaned in and offered me a deal. If I could help him pull between $6 million and $8 million of hidden assets from what was left of Southport, he said he'd split it with me.

I immediately volunteered.

But then Andrew seemed to reconsider. "On second thought, can't do it. You're too close to us," he explained.

"How about my buddy, Brad?" I ask. "We can trust him."

"No," Andrew kicked back. "Still too close."

Now for the record, Brad was a very close friend. He was also about as honest a person as I know. I'd never drag him or anyone I trusted into a mess like this. Not at least without full disclosure of what was really going on. After all, this was a criminal investigation. People were probably going to go to prison.

Also, even if I was stupid enough to ask him, Brad wouldn't say "yes." Of that, I was sure. But his was the first name that sprang into my head.

"We need a dummy third party to do it," Scherr said. "Someone with no connection to Southport."

I smiled at Andrew and assured him I was in. We shook hands and agreed to talk again soon. Andrew turned and walked away.

It was clear from that moment that this meeting wasn't really about the future of the vineyard. That was kabuki theater. This meeting was about harvesting the fraud.

As Andrew walked away, I texted Peter, "Done. Will walk around the block to you."

I didn't think it was a good idea to walk directly to where Peter and Donnie were sitting. For all I knew, Rob McGraw and Hugh Hill could be sitting right next to them. Walking what's called a "cleaning route" will allow me to see if it's safe to approach the federal agents.

I circled the block. Not only did I not see anyone from Southport, but Peter and Donnie had left their position as well. I began to head back to the garage when I spotted Peter walking in my direction with sunglasses on and a backpack over his shoulder. I just kept walking.

As we pass, Peter said just one word, "Garage."

So, there I was, standing inside a garage on Broad Street next to Chipotle Mexican Grille. Like magic, Peter showed up out of nowhere.

I gave him a nod—an unsaid "I'm okay." A few hours earlier, they had briefed me on what to do next.

I took the camera out of my backpack and put it on the top of a cement-filled pipe meant to keep cars away from the ticket booth. Peter quickly swept it up and put it in his backpack.

Then I did the same with each recording device. They were on the top of a cement-filled pole for less than a second before they disappeared into the FBI agent's bag.

Peter, who, with his sunglasses and backpack, could pass for a college student, looked at me, paused, and then turned around and walked out.

Not a word was spoken.

Moments later, my car arrives. I take off my sport coat, throw my bag in the back seat, tip the attendant, hop in, readjust the seat, plug "Vineyard" into the GPS, and drive off. My adrenaline is pumping full speed.

Not five minutes later, having broken numerous traffic laws, I'm heading north on the FDR Drive when the phone rings. It's Peter.

"Everything went really, really well, Richard. Great job!" he says.

I'm elated as well and bathing in the full-scale adrenaline rush. Peter and I talk for a few more minutes. He says he'll be back in touch in a day or so.

As I pull out of the Mid-Town Tunnel, I see nothing but open road in front of me. I've got a backache, but there's one feeling I can't get out of my head: That was a blast.

CHAPTER 41

Working with the FBI can be like walking a tight rope over the rim of a huge black hole.

On one side is how you got there—the slippery slope you walked to get to the edge where you first climbed on the rope. Looking back down, you can see, with astonishing clarity, how one wrong move, one slip of the lip, can blow up in your face. It's the mental image of you and your career tumbling back down that rocky hill if your employer finds out you're working for or with the FBI.

On the other side of that tight rope is the FBI—a big dark informational abyss. Information you provide goes in. Little to nothing comes back out. You have no idea what they're up to. You hear nothing. You see nothing. You know only what they want you to know.

So you convince yourself—at least I did—that if you do fall, the FBI will catch you. Somehow. It's nerve-wracking. Because you really have no idea.

Smart friends told me to leave this whole thing alone. Play it safe. Mind my own business and focus on the vineyard. Good advice. I ignored it.

Smart friends who are also very good lawyers warned me against taking this path. You never know what will happen once the government gets involved. He was right. It was great, spot-on advice.

But I ignored it. I was hooked.

***

By late September, I'm again talking to Peter several times each week. One day he tells me that his supervisor in Washington wants to meet me.

Not only that, but members of the task force want to come out to the vineyard for a "planning" session. Turns out, Andrew's dangle of $6 to $8 million in hidden assets got their attention. It's an opportunity they don't want to miss.

What am I going to say? No?

Tuesday, October 6, 2015

It's the simple things that trip you up. In this case, it was a completely simple, normal administrative blunder on my part.

My goal throughout my time at the vineyard was always to shield the Southport mess from the vineyard staff. I needed them to focus on doing their jobs the best they could.

The FBI and criminal stuff? I wanted that as far away from my key people as possible.

I didn't want anyone working at the vineyard to panic. Finding out the owners of your company were under FBI investigation… well, that might cause a few to start updating their resumés.

Lieb Cellars was on a roll now. We had completed a full rebranding of our product line. Our tasting room had undergone a rebrand. Gone was the bohemian, farm-stand vibe. Ami and her crew were now orchestrating a more upscale, more urbane, more sophisticated hospitality experience. With that came larger crowds and longer wait times. Bigger average check amounts too. The wine club, which provides critical cash flow in the slower off-season months, was growing rapidly as well. The place was humming.

People noticed too. Soon, other vineyards began approaching my top staffers, hoping to poach them. While that's kind of a compliment, their success could also mess you up badly.

Now, as you'll recall, CFO Dave, our CFO, is a Grade-A worrier. A great guy. But a first-class worrier. I don't mind. CFOs get paid to worry. But over the course of our years working together, he developed a distinctive habit.

See, I'd come down from Boston either on Monday night or Tuesday morning. I was by now a regular on the New London to Orient Point ferry. I knew the deckhands and cafeteria crew by name. And they knew mine.

Most Tuesdays, I took the 11:00 am ferry out of New London. That would put me at the vineyard house with about 30 minutes to spare before the weekly staff meeting—a sacrosanct event when you work for me.

Today, as I turned off Oregon Road and into the driveway of the Lieb House, I saw Dave's car and immediately knew there was a problem. Perhaps he wants to show me something in private before the meeting begins—something he wasn't comfortable telling me over the phone. It didn't happen often anymore. But in the early days, it was a regular occurrence.

I got out of my car and walked in the house. There was Dave sitting at the round dining room table where our meeting would take place.

Seeing Dave, I threw my travel bag at the foot of the stairs, made a quick pit stop, and sat down.

No greetings, no chit-chat, no small talk. Just Dave, looking a little more nervous than usual holding an envelope.

My first reaction was that he was resigning. I think I even made a joke like, "You quittin'?"

He answered, "No, but I need to know about this."

The "this" was a bill from one of the several law firms representing us. Specifically, it had a line item that read:

"Conversation w/ Bailey re: FBI Sting Operation-Southport—0.60 hours."

Oh boy. I guess that cat was out of the bag.

Big, big error on my part. I should have thought of this. But it was too late now. I had to think fast. What do I tell Dave, and... do I need to tell Ami and Russell too?

I never told the FBI this and thankfully, they never asked. But I decided that the smartest thing for me to do was trust these guys and give them a heads up.

So, I told them.

I didn't tell them everything. I didn't even tell them most of what was going on behind the scenes. But I needed them to know the big picture. If I didn't, and it leaked out some other way, they would have every right to turn their backs on me. So, I made the decision to trust them. It was a risk. But it was the right decision.

Yes, I said, the guys at Southport are in big trouble. It was clear to the FBI, our lawyers, and me (not that I matter) that a felony had been committed. Yes, the Southport guys may go to prison. And yes, I'm helping the FBI figure it all out. But no, this doesn't mean that the government is going to shut us down, which was their biggest fear. Rightly so.

I always believed that if I helped the FBI, it would only help the vineyard. I never saw the benefit in keeping my head down and ignoring a threat that could shut us down or kill us. I never thought, nor did I hope, that a process which I had no control over would quietly pass us by and leave us untouched. If there was going to be a conversation about the winery's survival, I wanted to be at that table with a few chits to call in. So, I pushed forward.

But I also read a little unstated concern on Ami, Dave, and Russell's faces. To them, I was a Southport guy. That's who hired me. That's how I got there. But all the things Southport was being investigated about? I told them that all the bad stuff had happened long before I ever heard of Southport Lane or knew there were vineyards on Long Island, which had the added benefit of being true.

We didn't do much regular business that day. I let them ask questions, and I tried to keep them focused on the future. The most productive thing we did was to make a plan.

Ever since *The Wall Street Journal* article appeared, I worried about the media. I feared that if reporters made the connection between Southport Lane and Lieb Cellars-Premium Wine Group, a media-feeding frenzy was likely.

This had all the bells and whistles of a killer story. Super rich people, vineyards, wine, the Hamptons, a fake Caravaggio, a 27-year-old self-proclaimed genius with a pretend Yale degree. Oh yeah, and at that time, what we thought to be $100 million in missing money.

While *The Wall Street Journal* did break the story nearly 18 months earlier, they took only a 50,000-foot snapshot. They didn't really care about the details. Their angle was lazy and, frankly, pretty superficial. To them, Alex Burns was a "wunderkind," a "financial prodigy," and now he was a bust.

They were right about the bust part. But a wunderkind and financial prodigy? That part was stupid.

Those of us who knew Alex knew he was neither. He was smart, yes. But not smart enough to connect all the dots his self-serving scheming created. But being right or correct wasn't critical to Alex. Impressing people was. Being a good liar or bullshitter was a hell of a lot easier. Faster too.

The *WSJ* writers never followed the vineyard angle. They did refer to it in one article, but they never dug any deeper, an omission for which I was deeply grateful.

So, for the balance of that day, I helped the three most important people in the business come to grips with the reality of the situation. I also outlined a simple plan meant to shield them from as much involvement as possible.

It was simple. If a member of the media or law enforcement called Dave, Ami, or Russell about the Southport folks, they were to tell them they had no idea about any of that, which again had the added benefit of being true, and then give them my phone number.

If I was unavailable, they were to refer them to Michael Weinstein. I gave them all Michael's number.

Michael's job in this communications strategy was to distance the vineyard from Southport. It was to define the degrees of separation between us at the vineyard and the folks at Southport Lane.

When *The Suffolk Times* called Russell Hearn, he referred the reporter to me. When the reporter called me, I referred him to Michael Weinstein. When he called Michael Weinstein, Michael went on the record and masterfully explained how the vineyard, and me, were multiple levels of separation from Southport.

I'd been an employee of Southport's for four months—January to April 2014. It wasn't a stretch.

I always thought that, if some reporter wanted to do a deep dive into this, the story would practically write itself. But no one did.

Grant Parpon at *The Suffolk Times* was the only one who made the connection between the vineyard and Southport Lane.

Our plan worked perfectly. Parpon says in his article that I deferred comment to Michael Weinstein. That was it.

We never heard from anyone in the media again.

Oh, and... after that planning session at the vineyard, I asked all our law firms to send their bills to my home outside of Boston. We had three separate law firms working for us at the time. They all sent their bills on the first week of every month.

Our poor mailman must have thought I was working for Whitey Bulger.

CHAPTER 42

That whole "the wheels of justice turn slowly" thing is the Gospel truth.

But once they begin to turn, look out! There's almost no chance of getting out of their way. You can't fight them. You can't outrun them. You can't hide from them. And you really can't bullshit your way past them.

You can try. But better than 90 percent of the time, you'll fail. Oh, and lying to a federal agent is a felony. That's what they got Martha Stewart for back in 2004. As a result, she did five months in federal prison.

As my brother Tom once told me, the Department of Justice is "the biggest law firm in the world." As my mother told me often when I was a kid, one of the secrets to success is to learn to "pick your battles."

Admittedly, I struggled with that motherly advice until I was in my late 40s or early 50s. Truth be told, I still struggle with it a little bit. I mean, how could a fight that felt right not be right? Right?

Perhaps. But that didn't mean you should fight. If only I'd grasped that nuance as a younger man.

But c'est la vie!

CHAPTER 43

It had now been four months since first meeting Peter and his investigative team. Back in June, it was a lot of nice "how do you dos." Not anymore. Over the course of the summer, the pace began to quicken. Our communications were now simple and straightforward. All business.

A month after my meeting in Southport's offices in lower Manhattan, my contacts with Peter and his team became almost daily.

Next on the government's agenda was a meeting at the vineyard. Peter said his boss wanted to meet me. He wouldn't say why.

***

During that time, it was pretty normal for employees of Lieb Cellars to stop over at the Lieb House. The four-car garage served as extra storage space and was filled with stuff. The wine cellar in the basement held our "Library Collection."

Sometimes a week would go by, and not a soul would stop by. Sometimes someone would visit several times a week. Or day.

If I wasn't at the Lieb tasting room or over at Premium Wine Group, I was generally to be found at the Lieb house, which doubled as my office.

Now, one of the upsides of letting Dave, Ami, and Russell in on the big secret is they completely understood when I said, "There's going to be a meeting here at the house next week. There can be no visitors. No matter how urgent. But if you absolutely need me, text me."

They're smart folks. No need for me to explain, and they knew better than to ask.

CHAPTER 44

October 14, 2015

It's 9:00 am sharp when two cars pull into the big circular drive-way at the vineyard house. Why are these guys always perfectly on time?

Five federal officers then get out. I recognize Peter and Don-nie—the IRS-CID guy. But the other three? No clue.

I'd run out earlier to my favorite deli to make sure I have fresh coffee and authentic NY bagels for them.

No one touched them, least of all me. I was too nervous.

They come in and sit at the big round table in the dining area. The conversation immediately begins with introductions. One guy, with a stern visage, doesn't give his name. He says he's a senior FBI agent based in Washington. Call it a hunch, but I'd be willing to bet he was the task force leader. He didn't speak much, but when he did, he did so with authority.

Two others—a male and a female—begin to introduce them-selves when the female stops mid-sentence. She looks over at the male and says, "Wait, what names are we using?"

"The usual," he says.

Think about that for a minute. You're sitting at a table with a bunch of federal agents when two agents have to decide what fic-titious names they're using.

The mere fact that they had that conversation in front of me told me two things:

1. They were obviously undercover agents.
2. I'd earned their trust.

That's pretty wild.

By the end of the meeting—at around 1:00 pm—they have an operational plan in place. My part is short, sweet, and simple.

I'm to introduce the undercover agents to Andrew. The story is they're a wealthy couple who live on a yacht currently docked near the vineyard. I've gotten to know them. They've been to the house and may want to rent it next summer, but I don't know them well, and I suspect they may be a little dodgy. So, they may be the perfect pair to help Andrew pull this mysterious $6 million to $8 million out of Southport.

Finally, they decide that the best way for me to make this introduction is to meet Scherr in person. They think a restaurant near where Andrew lives would be best. That way he's comfortable and on his own turf.

Everyone agrees on the plan. That done, the agents leave. They have planes to catch, and they need to get from the North Fork of Long Island all the way to JFK airport in Queens. It's about 72 miles—a good chunk of it on the dreaded and unpredictable Long Island Expressway.

It being early afternoon, I head over to the tasting room to let Dave and Ami know the coast is clear. Neither of them asks how it went. I just tell them my meeting is over.

They both look at me and say, "Okay. Cool."

Happy with how the day progressed, I went back to the vineyard house and tried to work. But my mind was wandering all over the place.

So when dinner time rolled around, I went to Greenport Harbor Brewing for a cheeseburger and a beer.

It was Trivial Pursuit night, and I love the game.

All's well that ends well, I guess.

CHAPTER 45

October 22, 2015
Bridgewater, NJ

A week later, I had a dinner scheduled with Andrew for 6:45 pm. He chose "Roots," a popular steakhouse in Morristown, New Jersey.

Following instructions, I meet Peter and Donnie at a Marriott 20 miles from Morristown, where we rehearse my part a few times.

I'm feeling confident now. No panic attacks. No flop sweats. For the most part, I know what to do and what to expect. I'm confident in my own abilities to stick with the script.

Peter explains that he and Donnie will be outside the restaurant... just in case.

He then reminds me that my sole objective tonight is to get Andrew to agree to meet Evan and Deirdre, the undercover agents. After that, I'm done. Enjoy a nice dinner on the FBI.

What he doesn't say is the FBI will be recording every word.

So much for a relaxing chat between colleagues.

Similar to the prep we did for the meeting at Southport's office, Peter then puts his index finger up to his lips in the universal "shh" symbol. Then he reaches into his backpack and pulls out two recording devices.

Being the old pro that I now am, I stick one in the same suitcoat pocket as I did a few weeks ago. The other goes straight into my shirt pocket.

He reaches into the backpack a third time and pulls out something completely different. It's a small rectangular pack—a lot like a jeweler's tool box. Except it has two to three wires hanging out of it.

It looks like a small improvised explosive device.

"This is a simultaneous transmitter," the veteran agent says. "We'll be listening to everything being said, in real time."

He stuck it in the inside pocket of my blazer.

"Make sure the wires are outside the pocket. It transmits better," he said.

Suddenly, I'm not so cocky and confident any more. I'm nervous. That old familiar pit returns to my stomach. I can feel beads of sweat forming on my forehead (or "fivehead" as my family jokingly calls it).

I don't know why. What's the difference between recording a conversation versus transmitting it? I'll tell you what. It's the wires hanging out of my suitcoat pocket.

That feels a little more dangerous. One wrong move. A scratch of my head. Reaching down to pick up a knife, a fork, or a napkin off the floor. Anything. The wires are likely to be noticed.

A million things could cause my jacket to open up. And there it would be, in plain view. Three to four wires hanging out of my coat pocket. How do you explain that away?

As on the day of the meeting at Southport's office, Peter and Donnie both stand up and shake my hand. It's time for me to go. No words are spoken.

I shake both their hands, turn around, and head for the door.

I'm on my own again.

***

Once I get in the car, turn the air conditioning on high (got to kill those beads of sweat on my "fivehead"), I plug the Roots address into my GPS, and pull out of the hotel parking lot.

I followed the GPS directions and drove straight to the restaurant. Morristown is a busy place. Finding a parking space is impossible. Luckily, I stumble on a municipal parking garage behind Roots. Though it's packed, I manage to find a space, hop out of the car, and head to the back door of the restaurant. It feels like I'm late. I hate being late.

At 6:21, I received a text from Peter: "Let me know when you arrive. We're in position." First thing that crosses my mind is, "How'd they beat me here?"

I walk in through the back door and head to the maître d' station up front. The place is pretty crowded. I look around. It's a typical Wall Street crowd. Most of the patrons are guys. Most are talking way too loud. Most are eating steaks the size of a Chihuahua. Most are also slugging down red wine in glasses the size of small fish tanks.

I've been to hundreds of client and team dinners like this over the past 30 years. New York, Chicago, Miami, Boston, Seattle, Los Angeles, Dallas, Houston, Denver, and a whole lot more. They're all the same. Trust me. There are enough lies being told and enough shit being slung to bust a million polygraphs.

But these dinners have a distinct purpose. The goal is to have a little fun. Talk a little smack. Toss in a little business.

But the real goal is much simpler. It's to finish the night with a stronger relationship with your client-partner-new friend than you had before dinner. This is it in a nutshell: Can you do business with them? Are they easy to deal with, or are they going to be a pain in the ass?

You find it all out over a Chihuahua and a gallon of good wine. Not to mention the one, maybe two martinis you had before you sat down. Thank God for expense accounts.

When I made the reservation, I requested a quiet table. Looking around, I realize that no such thing exists here. The maître d' sits me at a booth by the front door.

I immediately text Peter. "Seated by the door. Kinda loud."

Just as quickly he texts back, "We got it. Thanks."

After I sit down, the waiter comes over and asks me for a drink order. I tell him tonic water with a lime. Andrew, who hasn't yet arrived, doesn't drink much. I bet he won't have anything to drink tonight. He's way too disciplined.

At that moment, two men walk in the front door. They're clean-cut, in conservative suits, and look like they just got out of the shower after an easy five-mile run. They sit at the top of the bar within direct sight of my table. They keep glancing over at me.

I begin to wonder... is that another FBI team? If it is, great. Convinced that I'm being double-covered, I begin to relax.

A minute or two later, Andrew calls. He says he's eight minutes away. Good. We're still on.

Immediately, I text Peter, "He just called. Said he's 8 minutes away."

Peter texts back a simple, "Ok."

A few minutes later, Andrew walks in the front door.

***

My conversation with Andrew was productive. I told him the backstory on the two "investors." I told him that I ran a scenario by them—something sensitive—that a friend of mine (Andrew) "needed some help." Specifically, that he's looking for a "straw buyer" for some assets of a defunct private equity group.

My sense, I conveyed to Andrew, is that they may have financial problems. They seem to be well-off. But I don't think they actually are.

That would make them like so many of the people out on the east end of Long Island. They look like they're living large. But in reality, they're barely getting by.

Because of that, I said to Andrew, they may be the perfect patsies.

After hearing me out, Andrew says, "Set up the meeting."

My work is done. I sit back and try to enjoy a decent meal. Andrew and I talk about random stuff. Kids, the markets, etc…

It was an enjoyable conversation. I see a more human side of Andrew. A good husband. A good dad. I didn't feel the cold, transactional vibe he throws off in the office. He's smooth. He's polite. He's obviously smart.

For the first time, I find him rather likeable.

But when it comes to business, he just thinks differently than me. He goes somewhere I won't. To him, the rules are obstacles to get around, not boundaries that shouldn't be crossed.

That's where we differ. I'm a rules guy.

Opting out of the Chihuahua and gallon of red wine side of the menu, I ordered a piece of chicken with asparagus. Disciplined as ever, Andrew ordered some fish, which he barely touched. No wonder he's so thin. He's one of those guys that cuts up his food and moves it around his plate so it looks like he ate it.

Not me. I kill everything in sight. I'm suddenly nervous again. My mind is racing a mile a minute. I'm trying to slow my thought process down, so it catches up with my mouth.

Moreover, I'm thinking and rethinking whether what I just said to Andrew tipped my hand, all while trying to make friendly chit-chat.

At 8:55 pm, we're done. As I'm walking to the parking garage, I text Peter: "Done. Where do you want to meet?"

He gives me a one-word response: "Hotel."

On the 20-mile drive back to the hotel to meet Peter, a strange thing happened. It seems like the entire drive is one big, dark, windy road with very few streetlights. Suddenly, a car comes from no-where and starts following me very, very close to my rear bumper. His brights are on, and the glare is distracting.

I'm a little spooked, to say the least. I don't have a clue where I am. This doesn't look like the way I got there. My eyes are darting back and forth between the road in front of me and my new friend behind me.

So, I say out loud to no one in particular, or to everyone if they're listening: "I've had nothing to drink, and I'm definitely be-ing followed by a cop. Now, if he pulls me over, how do I explain the funny toys I'm carrying with me?"

See, if he pulls me over, I'm going to be very late checking back in with Peter at the hotel. That's going to set off some alarm bells.

Then a mile or two later, something else weird happens. The car following me pulls over to the side of the road and turns off its headlights. Out loud, I thanked everyone and anyone.

I get back to the hotel and knock on Peter's door. As he opens it, he gives me the "shhh" signal. I sit down and wait for him to fin-ish what he was doing. He closes his computer. I hand him all the devices he's planted on me. Within a minute, he's deactivated them.

Only then do we start talking.

"He'll do the meeting," I say. "But I got nothing else from him. Andrew is too disciplined. Too calibrated. Too controlled."

"You did fine, Richard," the agent says. "The goal was to get the meeting. You got it. So the night was a success."

But see, I feel like I failed. I wanted to get Andrew to talk about the whole scheme.

But Andrew is way too smart for that.

After giving him my summary of what happened, I feel like I fell short of the objective. Peter again says he's pleased with how the evening played out.

Done for the night, I go downstairs to the hotel bar. While sitting there, I see Donnie come in the front door and head to the elevators. He's clearly carrying take-out bags from some place.

I just had a fine meal on the government. These poor guys probably got something from a fast-food joint.

Oh well. Then I ordered a proper gin martini. Screw the tonic.

CHAPTER 46

A day or two later, Peter asked me to set up the meeting between Andrew and the two undercover agents. Andrew suggested a place in mid-town.

Even though I set it up, I wasn't invited—a fact that did not bother me in the slightest.

To this day, I haven't the faintest clue what happened at that meeting or what they discussed. Apparently, neither Andrew nor Peter felt I needed to know.

I'm okay with that. Know why? Because I have no choice.

When I asked if the meeting was productive, both Peter and Andrew gave the exact same response, "It went well."

And that is all I know.

***

In early December, Andrew informed me that he wanted to schedule a meeting at the vineyard. He wanted to bring Dean, Southport's Comptroller, along with him. The purpose was a financial review.

Now this set off all sorts of alarm bells for me. By this point, I'd been CEO of the vineyard companies for more than two years. Never once had Southport even asked for the financial statements. We had them. I now had trust in them, thanks to Dave's meticulous accounting. But they'd never expressed one iota of interest in our financial statements.

We still have enough cash in the bank to cover us through the winter. To top that off, we still have about $750 thousand from the debt that I'd guaranteed in November 2014.

We had used about $450,000 to buy some new tanks for the Premium Wine Group. That substantially expanded their ability to produce more wine. We paid off a lot of old accounts payable that had been running up over time. We funded operating losses from last winter and early spring.

But things were looking up. It was December, the slow season was upon us, and we had roughly $750,000 in the bank. We could cruise right through the winter doldrums.

But it was also clear to me Southport was struggling. They had moved to cheap offices in southern Manhattan. They had changed their name to Massive Interactive. They had even whittled themselves down to a skeleton crew. All signs of a decline in their good fortunes since Alex Burns had left nearly two years earlier.

My fear—and not an unreasonable one—was that they were coming for our cash. That they wanted to control it.

If that happened, I'd resign as President and CEO, not only of the parent company but of all three subsidiaries as well.

Now, if I resigned or was fired, my resignation would trigger a cascade of negative events. Let me explain.

I negotiated the loan package in the fall of 2014. Having agreed to personally guarantee the $2 million loan, I needed to protect myself. The last thing I wanted was for someone at Southport to decide to fire me for some idiotic reason. So, the lender and I agreed—and we put it into the loan document—that if I resigned or was fired, the loan would default.

That meant that they couldn't fire me without having $2 million—in either new debt or fresh cash—in their pockets to pay off the loan. Otherwise, the lender would call it.

Even better? No one would lend these guys money, except maybe the Mob, and the Mob is actually smarter than that.

Anyway, what bank is going to lend money to a group of guys trying to refinance a place they can't prove they own?

I'll tell you who. Nobody.

Remember, the Delaware Chancery Court awarded all the assets of Southport Lane to a Receiver. I knew this. Southport knew this. But Southport still claimed—in writing—that they were the "undisputed owners of 93 percent of the stock of Premium Beverage Group, the owner of all the vineyard entities."

It was a stupid claim. More stupid is that they put it in writing. But hey, I figured I'd play along. I'd participate in this silly little Kabuki theater. I still didn't see the need to pick a fight… yet.

While my buddy Jeff was no longer working for Southport, he was the only other member of the board of Premium Beverage Group besides me.

At the time we borrowed the money, "the board" gave me a very healthy employment contract. I abstained from the vote, of course. But the contract stated that if they fired me, they would owe me two years' salary.

I asked our local attorney—Morgant Fiedler—to review and approve all the documents—the loan agreements, the minutes of the board meeting, and my employment contract. Before signing anything, I sent a copy of everything to Southport. Hugh, Southport's in-house counsel, said something simple and direct: "We're in the asset preservation business, not the asset liquidation business. Do what you have to do."

So, I did.

To this day, I bet they never read the documents. In November 2014, they had bigger problems. But at least I had the paper trail to cover my ass.

December 15, 2015

Andrew and Dean were due to arrive at the vineyard at around noon for the "financial review."

When I told Peter about Andrew's desire to meet at the vineyard, he immediately sensed an opportunity. He asked me if I was willing to be wired up for the meeting.

"In for a penny, in for a pound," I told him, echoing what I told Michael Weinstein six months earlier when he first asked if I'd wear a wire.

Peter said he couldn't make it that day because he had other commitments, but he would try and find another agent to cover me.

The next morning, he called me with the plan.

An agent named Tim would meet me as I got off the boat in

Orient Point, New York. He would wire me up. He would also show me how to deactivate the devices, which I had to do after Andrew and Dean left. The next day, I was to meet Peter and Donnie in Manhattan, where I'd return the devices.

He asked me where we should meet. I chose the bar of the Roosevelt Hotel, directly across the street from Southport's old offices at 350 Madison Ave.

For me, that was a nice touch of irony.

When I got there at around 11:30 am, Dean, the comptroller, was already there. Andrew was still driving out. He lives in New Jersey. Getting around New York City and then driving the full length of the Long Island Expressway can be a hassle.

So when I walked into the vineyard's offices, Dean was waiting in the conference room-wine library.

My original intent was to prep Dean a little bit. But I also saw this as a great opportunity to get his read on everything. As I pulled out my chair to sit down, I said, "You know, ever since *The Wall Street Journal* article, people here are nervous being around you guys."

Clearly caught off guard, Dean leaned back in his chair and looked at me quizzically. His expression changed. Then he explained Southport's purpose and reasoning behind transaction after transaction. He made sure to explain how they were structured to touch all the right legal bases, though some of them were "questionable."

He seemed proud of it all. Like it was a demonstration of intellectual and financial sophistication. It wasn't a confession by any means. It was a boast.

And I got it all on tape.

***

The next day, at the Roosevelt Hotel, I met with Peter and Donnie.

As I walked them through the events of the day before, the usually unemotional IRS agent broke into a big grin. "It's always the bookkeeper," he said. "Every time."

We all laughed.

But for me, I had a feeling of finality—that my part was complete. I can't articulate it, but I could sense that my job was done.

I'd spent months and thousands of dollars trying to get to the right person at the FBI. I provided original evidence in the form of the bank statements and other documents. I assisted them in every way they asked.

And I kept the vineyard alive and growing. No one missed a paycheck.

Yet, for the next three weeks, the call activity between Peter and me seemed to proceed at a frenzied pace.

New Year's Eve, New Year's Day, and nearly every day for a while after, the calls, though brief, continued to come. A quick question here, requests for someone's phone number there. Have you ever heard of this person or that person?

Finally, Peter asked me for a layout of Southport's offices in their new building downtown. Where are the doors? The filing cabinets? Whose offices belong to whom?

All this time I was keeping Michael Weinstein informed of each step, each call.

A day or two after New Year's, Michael said to me, "Richard, the government is on the move."

Boy was he right.

January 14, 2016, 3:00 pm

My buddy Jeff can be amazing. At around 3:00 pm, he called me. I was out at the vineyard preparing to head back to Boston.

"Hey... you know my friend George, who has an office across from Southport downtown?"

"Sure." I'd met George a couple of times through Jeff. A good guy, a pretty smart guy.

"Well," Jeff continued, "he just called me. Apparently, there are a bunch of FBI and IRS agents at Southport's office. They're lugging out boxes of stuff and computer shit."

Frankly, I felt pretty stunned. The thing is, as you're going through all this, you never know how it's going to end.

I knew this day was coming, but now that it was here, I wasn't quite sure what to think of it.

I thanked Jeff and jumped off the phone. He probably thought

I was an ingrate or something. But after all the wild events of the previous two and a half years, I did the only thing that made sense: I called Michael Weinstein.

Michael could tell I was a bit shaky. So he calmly and patiently explained what had happened to get to this point. And what, most likely, was coming next.

He explained that in order to raid Southport's offices, Peter and the task force had to get a search warrant. A federal judge or magistrate had to sign that warrant. That means they had to prove to the judge they had probable cause to believe that a felony had been committed.

He also explained, for my benefit, that if they had gone this far, then the government thought they had clear and convincing evidence that a crime had been committed. If not, they wouldn't have made the request to the judge.

A few weeks later, *The Wall Street Journal* published an article on the raid. I don't know where they got the information. I never spoke to them.

A dozen FBI and IRS agents executed a search warrant on Southport's offices that day. During the raid, they seized roughly 20 boxes of records as well as numerous computer hard drives.

In a document filed with the court during the criminal discovery process, the government stated that they turned over to the defendants more than eight million pages of documents.

After the January 14th raid, Rob McGraw called Peter and met him that very same day at Peter's hotel. Rob wanted to "explain" to the government what really happened. According to Rob's sentencing submissions, Peter thanked him for the information and said he would get back to him. Rob pled guilty to one count of fraud and was sentenced to 18 months in prison.

Andrew Scherr would later be sentenced in Dallas to 60 months in prison.

Driving home after the raid on January 14, 2016, I felt numb.

CHAPTER 47

Before he was Alexander Chatfield Burns, private equity man-child, Wall Street prodigy, vineyard owner, and always the self-proclaimed "smartest person in the room," he was Lexy Burns at Colleytown Elementary and Middle School in Westport, Connecticut.

At Colleytown, where Lexy was in the gifted and talented program, a contemporary described him "as a chameleon. Always trying to impress people. We hung out once or twice but never at his house, always mine."

It was there, according to Dan Woog, a lifelong Westporter and publisher of the blog-website 06880danwoog.com, that Lexy's life as a serial imposter seemingly began to take shape.

According to Woog's site, one mother recalled Lexy as being "brilliant—really 'out there' smart" at Colleytown Middle. She added: "I think he may have won a huge award for coming up with some new idea having to do with fuel or gas or something. It was a big deal in the science world."

Lexy Burns as a high school junior
roughly 2003-2004
(Source: 02880danwoog.com)

According to 06880, Burns grew up in Westport and was known as "a financial prodigy."

"When he was about 13," his mother told Robert N. Gordon, a friend and head of Twenty-First Securities Corp., "Lexy determined that a famed options-pricing model was wrong and "he had a better idea. The model, called Black-Scholes, had won its authors a Nobel Prize.

Once, Alex told me—and apparently several others—that not only did he find the error in the Nobel Prize winning Black-Scholes Option Pricing Model, but also, while in high-school, he developed his own "Monte Carlo" simulation.

A Monte Carlo simulation is a model used to predict mathematical outcomes while factoring in random variables. If your model works, it basically allows you to predict the future with a certain degree of mathematical probability.

We can only assume, like the Black-Scholes story, there was no Monte Carlo simulation. But that didn't stop him from telling middle school friends he could execute multi-million-dollar trades from his school computer.

Around this time (2001), when Lexy was about 14 and a freshman in high school, the movie "A Beautiful Mind" was released.

While there's no way of knowing this for certain, I think Lexy latched onto the story about John Nash, the Nobel Laureate from Princeton, and incorporated parts of Nash's life into his own.

John Forbes Nash Jr, was a proponent of game theory—a novel way of looking at markets and finance. Socially awkward (which Alex Burns certainly was) and suffering from mental health issues—Alex's coroner's report specifically mentions him suffering from Asperger's Syndrome—Nash overcame his mental health issues to win the Nobel Prize in Economics in 1994.

Both John Nash and Alex Burns covered the windows of their workspaces with formulas and equations.

When the movie came out in 2001, I suspect that the insecure but bright, precocious high school freshman named Lexy Burns empathized deeply with the character on the big screen played by Russell Crowe.

Also, around that time, Lexy's mother married a gentlemen named Roger Chatfield. Lexy, though not formally adopted by Roger Chatfield, soon took on Chatfield as his middle name.

A middle school friend of Lexy told me he had no recollection of Lexy graduating from Staples, the local public high school. "In fact," the friend told me, "he kinda disappeared. I have no idea where he went to college."

By the time I met Alex in 2013, he claimed Mayflower ancestry through the Chatfield line, and the windows in his office, like John Nash's, were covered with formulas and equations.

And, no one at Southport ever made mention of "Lexy Burns."

It was at Southport Lane where all his hopes and dreams could come together. Here, he was in charge. He was in control. If people questioned him, he would remind them—as he often did—that he was "the smartest person in the room."

And guess what? It worked. He hired journeyman financiers and brokers, or as a Southport consultant, friend, and Harvard MBA once remarked to me, "not exactly the A-team of finance."

But Alex paid these journeymen well enough so that they didn't dare ask impertinent questions. All needed Alex on their side if they were going to collect a huge fee on the deals they were trying to bring to Southport Lane.

As a result, his reinvention as the personification of old Yankee money and Nobel Prize-level intellect came together at Southport Lane, which he bragged had "over a billion dollars in commitments."

After all, it's New York City. The ultimate meritocracy. Who would know?

***

The New York financier's life was good to Alex. He soon started flying by private jet. Beautiful women appeared on his arm at charity functions. Buying a vineyard on the East End of Long Island added to the mystique. He even drove a black Porsche 911 convertible sporting the vanity license plate, "Reinsure."

But it didn't last. It couldn't.

The torrent of lies, the multiple fraudulent transactions—all caught up with him in January 2014. That's when, across the table from me and staring down at his phone, he said, "Oh fuck, oh fuck, oh fuck. I hate my insurance companies."

I think that was the moment when he realized it was all about to collapse. All the lies were about to be exposed. Alexander Chatfield Burns would soon be known as a fraud.

So, he got up and walked out the door, never to be seen by any of us again.

He checked himself into Bellevue's psych ward and texted his girlfriend, "I had a nervous breakdown."

According to court documents, he was at Bellevue for one day. Then he went home to his mother in Westport, CT.

***

But he wasn't done yet. Not even close.

Lexy may have moved back to Mom's after the setback at Southport, but a few months later, Alexander Chatfield Burns re-emerged, this time in the beautiful, historic, and genteel southern city of Charleston, South Carolina.

As best I can tell, no one knew him there. He could start life all over again.

It helped that Alex also had a little extra money in his jeans.

Toward the end of Alex's time at Southport—think the end of August 2014—his management company "Raubritter LLC" (remember, in German, Raubritter translates as "Robber Baron") collected a tidy sum from the Kingdom of Denmark.

How? Simple, if you have no problem filing false tax returns.

It seems that prior to leaving Southport, Alex met two high-brow grifters who explained to him a little loophole in Danish-U.S. tax law.

It worked like this: If you are a U.S. pension fund, buy and sell shares on the Danish Stock Market, and make a profit, you're going to be charged a capital gains tax on those profits. But the question then becomes: To which country do you pay—Denmark or the U.S.?

When you sell a stock and make a profit in Denmark, the Danish government withholds an amount from the sale equal to the capital gains tax due the Danish government.

Under a tax treaty with the United States, instead of paying the Danish government the amount of the capital gains tax they would normally withhold from profits made in Denmark, that amount was refunded to U.S. pension investors so they could pay U.S. capital gains taxes.

See, all you had to do to get sent a check was fill out a Danish capital gains form and submit it to the Danish tax office known as *Skattestyrelsen*, better known as "SKAT." In it, you listed your buy price, your sell price, and ultimately your profit.

You then verified you were an eligible pension fund and *voila!* They sent you a check for the capital gains tax they believed—incorrectly—they had withheld upon the sale of the stock.

And being the kind, trusting souls that the Danish regulators must be, they didn't mail those payments to the U.S. government. They mailed them directly to the investor.

Thus, a little cottage industry of fraud was born.

Before catching on to this nefarious little loophole, more than 140 companies were refunded more than $2 billion in stock trades that never actually took place.

Among them was Raubritter LLC Pension Plan.

Starting in late 2013 and ending in August 2014, Raubritter LLC Pension Plan had submitted over $9,000,000 in requests for reimbursement from SKAT. Each request was signed by Alexander Chatfield Burns.

According to court documents, and pursuant to an agreement with the two people who not only introduced him to this scam but shepherded the paperwork through SKAT, Alex pocketed a cool $900,000 merely for lending Raubritter's name and Alex's signature to the scheme.

Charleston, South Carolina must have been looking pretty good to Alex. Southport Lane and all those problems were clearly behind him. Or at least so he thought.

He was in a fun new town. No one knew of his New York history, and he had a nice little pile of cash to play with.

He must have thought himself pretty smart. Once again.

While writing this book, I was contacted by many, many people affected by the Southport fraud. Most knew Alex and Andrew and wanted to share their stories. Some were friends. Some co-workers. Some former bosses. Some, believe it or not, were family members.

Quite frankly, everyone I spoke with, be they friends, family, or former co-workers of Alex and Andrew, had variations of the same emotional conflict. Nearly all thought Alex was an out-and-out liar. But he could also be kind, funny, and generous. So, they let the lies slide.

My wife and I were in Charleston for a long weekend—neither of us had ever been there—and after a long day walking around the downtown area and visiting Ft. Sumter, she had no problem if I met up with a couple of Burns' friends who'd contacted me months before. We met at the bar in our hotel.

They were nice guys. Normal guys. Fun to talk to and hang out with. Both knew Alex pretty well. One had even done some work with him.

Early in the conversation, I asked one of them, "How did you meet Alex?"

"I met him at a poker game," one responded. "I don't remember who invited him, but when one of the guys asked Alex what he did for a living, Alex replied gruffly, 'I'm retired.'

"Most of the guys thought he was kind of a jerk," the friend added, "but I found him interesting. He could be funny. We even became friends. I went to his bachelor party and his wedding."

When sitting at the poker table that night passing himself off as a wealthy retiree, Alex Burns was all of 27 years old.

I believe—from talking to his friends there—that in Charleston, Alex Burns tried to go normal. I mean as normal as you can be when you are 27, retired after having stripped multiple insurance companies of $350 million, and are in a place where nobody knows you and you have at least a million or more dollars of swindled cash stashed away.

***

Back in New York, the initial shock of Alex leaving Southport brought on an eerie quiet from the folks at 350 Madison Ave. The only real communication with them was when they needed something. As the new CFO Bob Yingling said to me once, "We're just waiting for the liquidators to show up."

A few months later, Bob left. Smart guy.

But oddly enough, nothing happened. From what I could piece together, the insurance companies were up in arms at Burns. It was clear to them that money was missing. Nobody seemed to know how much. But from my short distance away at the vineyard, it seemed like nothing was going on. It seemed that way for the better part of 2014 and into 2015.

My understanding was that Hugh was dealing with all that crap. He was trying his best to satisfy angry creditors and keep the consequences of the fraud from spreading to the rest of the Southport world. Frankly, it was an impossible task. But he managed it for more than a year.

With the exception of my occasional calls with Andrew or Hugh, everybody just left me alone.

I knew where $25 million had gone. I had the bank statements. I even tried to help them out. I sent them my excel spreadsheet prepared for the "Shit I Did" meeting. But I never heard back from them.

So, imagine my surprise when, a few years later, the lawyers for the insurance company sent me a batch of documents, prepared by Southport Lane for me to verify. Among them was the "Shit I Did" spreadsheet. As if Southport had created it.

Typical.

My phone calls to Hugh, Andrew, and Rob McGraw frequently went unreturned. E-mails asking for opinions, information, or guidance were frequently met with a simple, "Thx." No further response. But to be honest, they had other—more "pressing"— matters on their minds.

Only my pal Jeff responded. But it was clear he was making plans to move on from Southport. At least I could trust Jeff to give me an honest answer.

I threw myself into keeping the vineyard alive by pleading with Andrew Scherr, now the sole owner of Southport, to follow through on the $250,000 commitment Alex had made to the vineyard and me shortly after Alex had walked out.

Andrew insisted I prepare a plan complete with financial projections. So I did.

He reviewed it and called me one afternoon. "Okay," he said, "we'll send you the money. But that is it. No more. You are on your own out there" (meaning the east end of Long Island).

Shortly thereafter, he laid me off from Southport. "If you want to continue getting paid," he stated, "you'll have to figure that out yourself."

That was the best news I'd had in a while. I was on my own. In charge and with minimal oversight. Now I could move this company in the right direction without interference from people who had no idea how to run a business.

I was psyched.

***

Within weeks of arriving in Charleston, Alex had cultivated the persona of a rich, young baron of the New York hedge fund world who'd escaped the madness of Manhattan for the quieter, more relaxing life of a southern gentleman.

No longer had he gone to Yale. Now, he was a Columbia grad. He'd taken some courses there—in the School of Continuing Education. So at least he could talk the talk if he met someone with more than a passing knowledge of New York's Ivy League university.

But, like a true addict, the persona he cultivated proved impossible to maintain.

Just as he did at Southport Lane, Alex loved to create complex organizational charts filled with intermediary limited liability companies that had little or no value. Like a lot of people I've met, Alex equated complexity with smart.

Not me. I always try to simplify things.

In November 2014, State Acquisitions LLC, a company he set up only five months earlier, created seven separate wholly-owned subsidiaries. Then, each of the subsidiaries of State Acquisitions LLC acquired the assets of seven Church's Fried Chicken Restaurants in and around Charleston, SC.

Mimicking Southport all over again, he created State Acquisitions LLC in Delaware. He also formed a management company, Hamilton Associates LLC, to enter into an agreement with each separate Church's Fried Chicken company to provide management services, for which Alex's companies would be paid management fees.

In short, he created the exact same complex structure he had in New York. Instead of using highly regulated insurance companies, he did it with unregulated fried chicken restaurants.

A friend who knew Alex at the time said "he bought seven Church's Fried Chicken locations. Some sight unseen."

Within two years, many of the individual locations had been closed. In 2018, he was up to his ears in lawsuits, evictions, and claims that mandatory franchise fees had gone unpaid for months. So he closed all of the locations.

Somehow, though, Alex managed to afford a lovely, $1 million house in the well-to-do Charleston suburb of Mt. Pleasant.

During this time, he even managed to get on national TV for one of his other ventures.

In 2016, a segment of "CBS This Morning," anchored by Norah O'Donnell and broadcast nationally, opened with:

O'Donnell:

"Fans of aged alcohol may want to celebrate a big disruption in the spirits industry. Bottles of older scotch, bourbon, or rum can cost hundreds or even thousands of dollars, but one man is changing all that with an invention he claims can produce the equivalent of a 20-year-old spirit in less than a week.

Reporter (CBS News correspondent Ben Tracy):

Charleston, South Carolina, is a town that likes its carriages horse-drawn, its streets cobble-stoned, and its rum barrel-aged.

So when Alex Burns recently opened the Rational Spirits Distillery in Charleston, his business plan seemed a little—well, *irrational*: make rum that tastes old, but without any barrels, reports.

"The reason [there are] no barrels is because you have this" [Burns, on camera, talking].

"This machine—this is our science fair project," Burns said.

He's talking about a reactor, which looks like something you might find in a bio-tech lab, not a rum factory.

[Burns talking]"I came across this article that says, 'Guy claims he can create 20-year-old rum in six days,' and I thought to myself, 'Wow, that would solve a lot of problems! Lemme check it out!'"

There on national TV was Alexander C. Burns extolling the virtue of his new rum brand, Santeria. There was even footage of Santeria priests blessing the rum.

***

But as with most things Alex, the relationship devolved into accusations of misrepresentations and ultimately lawsuits.

In the court documents, Alex's former partners say he frequently described himself as a rich Wall Street guy who could afford to fund Rational Spirits and Santeria Rum until they became profitable.

To prove it, he flew his new friends and partners to football games on "his private jet."

He even managed to get them to build the "Alexander C. Burns" library for his personal wine collection.

Alex even went to law school for a year. But as his friend told me, "After *The Wall Street Journal* articles came out, Alex realized that his chances of being admitted to the South Carolina bar—or any bar, for that matter—were slim to none."

So, he quit.

CHAPTER 48

In September 2017, Sydney Alexis ("Alix") Barret married Alexander Chatfield Burns.

Ms. Barrett didn't know it at the time, but she had already become the final victim of a series of Alex Burns frauds over almost a decade.

A full year before they got married, Alex Burns offered to pay for Alix Barrett to attend graduate school at Clemson. Ms. Barrett consented. After all, they were going to be married and he was a retired "Wall Street" guy. He could afford it.

But by that time, the sins of Southport Lane were catching up with him. Not only was he being investigated by the FBI, DOJ, IRS, and SEC, but he was also a defendant in numerous state and federal lawsuits filed by the insurance companies and state regulators affected by the Southport fiasco.

His life was clearly unravelling. He must have been swamped with legal bills. Always confident he could scheme his way out of things, Alex Burns came up with one more fraud designed to pay his wife's graduate school tuition and keep up his charade as a man of great wealth.

Enter Discover Bank, the wholly-owned subsidiary of Discover Financial Services—owners of the popular Discover credit card.

Discover Bank had a student loan division. Not only that, but its loan application process was done completely online. No pictures, no meetings. The process was designed to be easy and smooth. In fact, to apply, all you needed was:

- Social Security number (if applicable)
- School information, including field of study and academic period of enrollment

- Loan amount requested, as well as any financial aid you expected to receive
- Financial information, including income and monthly mortgage/rent payments (if applicable)
- Permanent address and temporary/in-school address

Sounds easy, right?

So, in 2016, Alex filled out the online form in hopes of financing his fiancée's graduate education. Only he did so using the name "Sydney Barrett," even though she'd gone through life exclusively as "Alix Barrett."

Alex found there was also some money to be made.

Under the guise of financing your fiancée's education, you put a little cash in your pocket. Sounds like a pretty sweet deal.

For each of the student loans that Alex Burns applied for through Discover Bank using his fiancée's information, he engineered it so he would receive a portion of the requested funds by way of a refund from Clemson University.

He could nicely offset a few legal bills that way. Those refunds were directly deposited to an account he kept hidden from his fiancée (later his wife). The remaining portion of the funds was retained by Clemson University and applied to Ms. Barrett's tuition.

Not bad.

Alex Burns took out four loans in the name of Sydney Barrett for a total of $86,303.77. All without his fiancée's/new bride's ever knowing.

CHAPTER 49

Apparently, prior to marrying Alex Burns, Alix Barret never Googled her new husband. If she had, she would have saved herself a whole lot of heartache.

In October 2018, Alex was charged by the SEC of defrauding Southport Lane's advisory clients and pocketing millions in fees. He quickly consented to an SEC judgment, which, like all SEC judgments, was widely publicized.

Alix Barret Burns knew nothing of her new husband's history of fraud until October 2018. Upon discovering the depths of his past activities, she slowly began the process of divorcing him.

CHAPTER 50

Alex Burns was last seen alive at around 1:00 pm on October 26, 2021. He had been living with his girlfriend—not his wife—in a luxury apartment not far from downtown Charleston. The divorce was not yet final.

Unknown to all of us, Alex Burns, in November 2018, had pled guilty in U.S. District Court for the Southern District of New York to eight separate counts of fraud related to the $350 million fraud at Southport Lane.

From 2018 to 2021, all court records on the case remained under seal while Alex cooperated with the Justice Department in the criminal cases against his old partner Andrew Scherr and financial whiz Rob McGraw.

According to public records, on October 25, 2021, Alex received a piece of significant news regarding a "legal matter" he had been dealing with for years. What few people knew—because it was still under seal—is that Alex Burns was informed then that he would be sentenced on December 12, 2021 for the crimes he admitted to back in 2018.

Part of the criminal sentencing process involves the prosecution and defense submitting to the judge what are known as "Pre-Sentencing Reports" or "PSRs."

A PSR presents the findings of an investigation in the context of the "legal and social background" of a person convicted of a crime. Its purpose is to determine if there are extenuating circumstances which should influence the severity or leniency of a criminal sentence. Judges heavily rely upon them when considering a sentence.

According to the U.S. Sentencing Guidelines, which are not mandatory but advisory, the prosecution probably recommended a sentence of at least 15 years in prison.

While all judges view sentencing differently, the negative news Alex received on October 25, 2021 may have been the prosecution's recommendation of a lengthy prison sentence, despite his prior cooperation with them.

According to the Coroner's report, Alex's girlfriend left their apartment to run errands around 1:00 pm. When she returned, she found Alex lying shirtless on their bathroom floor. His lips, fingers, and toes were blue. He was dead. She immediately dialed 911.

EMS responded within minutes. They confirmed his death at 2:55 pm. The cause of death was listed as "Asphyxia due to methemoglobinemia due to sodium nitrite toxicity. Ketamine toxicity was listed as contributory." The manner of death was deemed "suicide."

A glass of yellowish liquid was found on the bedroom nightstand.

In a quirk of the law, because he died before being sentenced, the government had no choice but to file a motion declining further prosecution and dropping all charges. This was and is customary under these circumstances.

Thus, despite millions still unaccounted for, Alexander Chatfield Burns died an innocent man.

A few weeks later, Sydney Alexis Barrett Burns found out she owed Discover Bank more than $86,000.

EPILOGUE

"Rob structured the deals and Burns sold the lie."

That statement, made to me in a telephone call taped and given to the FBI in July 2015, sealed everyone's fate. It was an admission that a crime—a felony—was known to have taken place at Southport Lane.

From that point on, I never doubted that people were going to go to prison. I just didn't know who, when, for how long, or where.

It also gave me a little peace that I was doing the right thing. That I wasn't a "snitch." I confess that I struggled with that notion. In the nine months from when I first approached my FBI neighbor—with evidence that would later show up in the indictment—until the first time I met with Peter and his investigative team at Michael Weinstein's office in June 2015, I thought about that quite a bit.

It was Mike Ciravolo at Bo Deitl's office who clarified it for me. "Richard," he said, "a snitch is someone who actively participates in the crime and then sells out the other guys to try and avoid going to prison. That's not you. You're one of the good guys."

I can't tell you how much that conclusion, coming from him, meant to me.

After my first meeting with the FBI team, it was a race to get enough information for a grand jury to return an indictment. On April 24, 2019, three years and nine months later, a grand jury empaneled in Dallas, Texas, secretly indicted Robert E McGraw III and Andrew B Scherr on seven counts of insurance and wire fraud.

On page 7, paragraph 26 appears the statement that the victim insurance companies were purchasing, among other things, "(iii) 4 percent loan payments issued to Premium Wine Acquisitions that were secured by real property and agricultural equipment."

But there was only one problem: It wasn't true. From the time I first set foot on the property in April 2013 up until the time I borrowed $2 million dollars in November 2014, all the assets of Premium Wine Acquisitions were free of all liens and encumbrances. There were no loans. No interest payments. The first I heard of all that was when Rob McGraw called me out of the blue to ask how I was going to repay the $25 million.

For me, the most satisfying part of the indictment appears on page 8, paragraph(s) 27 and 28. In those two paragraphs are the exact figures I presented to Alex Burns in August 2013. The ones he decided to explain away by calling them "Shit I Did." I turned that exact Excel spreadsheet over to the FBI in my very first meeting in October 2014. They had it. In Alex's original handwriting. "Shit I Did."

Rob McGraw was arrested by the FBI at his apartment in Long Island City (the Borough of Queens or the "City of Ashes" for you *Great Gatsby* fans) on May 2, 2019. The arresting agent wasn't Peter or any agent I'd met along the way. Apparently, the FBI assigns tasks like that to the nearest field office. So, it's not like in the movies or on TV when the dogged investigator gets to knock on the door, confront the perp, and then read him his Miranda rights as he's slapping on the cuffs. But Rob did get a knock on the door. That must have been a terrifying moment. He was released later that day on personal recognizance.

Andrew Scherr was always the smartest of the bunch. He was cool, calm, calibrated, and cerebral. Until he enticed me to help him pull $6 million to 8 million in hidden assets out of Southport, I cannot think of a single time when he ever let on that he was in the middle of a $350 million fraud. When we did discuss it, he steadfastly asserted that it was all Alex, and it all caught him by surprise too. I never believed that. But he stuck with it. I told Peter this on any number of occasions. Andrew was tightly wrapped and always in control.

Unlike Rob, who was arrested at home, Andrew flew down to Dallas and turned himself in. I can only believe that by doing so he spared his family the spectacle of being led away in handcuffs in front of them. If that is true, I respect that.

Andrew was arraigned in federal court in Dallas on May 7, 2019, a full five days after the FBI showed up at McGraw's apartment. After being arrested, arraigned, and processed, he was allowed to fly home to New Jersey.

On the night of May 2, 2019, lead agent Peter called me to tell me the indictments had been unsealed, and arrests were in the process of being made. I'd imagined this moment for nearly four years now. This is what it was all about.

But I felt no joy. I felt no sense of accomplishment. I knew deep down that I'd done the right thing and was glad I'd done it. But I couldn't imagine what these guys that I knew and worked with were going through. I knew they were guilty. But I felt horrible, nonetheless. Primarily, I felt horrible for their families.

During all this, I'd become a PACER addict (PACER stands for "Public Access to Court Electronic Records.") It's also the official medium of the U.S. Federal Courts to file all sorts of motions, answers, letters, etc…

For the next seven to eight months, I checked PACER three to four times per day. The minute something was filed, I downloaded it. At a cost of $0.10 per page, I began to ring up quite the bill. But I was a PACER addict, and addicts don't care.

Rob McGraw's attorneys were filing motions to be tried not in Dallas, where the indictment was filed, but back in New York. I mean, it made perfect sense. That's where he and Andrew lived. But it was on December 31, 2019 that Andrew's attorneys stated in a filing that he was in "advanced plea negotiations with the government."

Just four days later, on January 3, 2020, Andrew's legal team filed a "Factual Resumé" in which Andrew admitted his guilt to the crimes committed while at Southport. It was signed by Andrew, his attorney, the U.S. Attorneys' Office in Dallas, and two representatives of the U.S. Department of Justice. Included in paragraph 26 is information I came across in preparation for the "Shit I Did" meeting and provided to the FBI in October 2015 and in June 2016.

On January 24, 2020—after Andrew's guilty plea was entered into the record—the United States District Court for the Northern District of Texas granted Rob McGraw's motion to transfer his case back to the Southern District of New York for trial.

Then the world shut down over COVID. But that didn't do much to stop the glacial yet inexorable grind of the U.S. Department of Justice. As we all have learned, you can get an amazing amount of work done with little more than e-mails and the new must-have, Zoom.

Rob pled guilty on August 20, 2020, to one count of fraud. In 2012, he had sent an e-mail to Southport's custodial bank that $50 million in Beaconsfield Securities deposited in that bank in the name of Dallas National Insurance were in fact genuine and worth the $50 million. The problem was, he, Andrew, and Alex had only created Beaconsfield Securities a few days before. In fact, it was worth nothing. That e-mail and the activities leading up to it ruined Rob's promising career and impressive reputation. Forever.

By convincing the bank that they were genuine, Rob and the crew had fulfilled the requirement of the Texas Department of Insurance that they deposit $50 million into Dallas National Insurance, thereby shoring up the company's financial health.

Now firmly in control of Dallas National, they changed the company's name to Freestone Insurance and transferred the corporate domain of the company from Texas to Delaware. Shortly thereafter, they managed to sell another $25 million in equally fictitious securities to the newly capitalized Freestone Insurance. To pay for them, Freestone Insurance wired $25 million at Southport's discretion to their nominee bank.

Of that $25 million, $7 million disappeared, and the balance of $18 million was immediately transferred to the account of…. wait for it…. Premium Wine Acquisitions Inc. at First Republic Bank— the very same bank account whose statements were provided to me in July 2013, and which became the basis of my preparation for the "Shit I Did" meeting in August 2013.

Having pled guilty, both Rob and Andrew now entered the sentencing phase of their cases. Shortly after pleading guilty, Andrew apparently suffered a heart attack that required quintuple bypass surgery. The court, in its mercy, postponed his sentencing several times.

Both Rob's and Andrew's attorneys also filed motions indicating their wish for the sentencing hearings to be conducted in person and not over Zoom. With the Department of Justice's agreement, the court then set multiple dates for sentencing.

The problem was, federal courthouses were still shuttered due to the pandemic, so "in the interest of caution" and "to serve the cause of justice," they postponed the sentencing hearings some more.

But time and tide wait for no man.

On June 16, 2021, U.S. District Judge Katherine Polk Failla in the Federal Courthouse in Manhattan sentenced Robert E Mc-Graw III to 18 months in prison and ordered to pay restitution in the amount of $50 million.

Just two months later on August 6, 2021 in Dallas Texas, U.S. District Court Judge Karen Gren Scholer sentenced Andrew Scherr to 60 months in prison followed by another five years of supervised release. And he was ordered to pay a total of $286 million in restitution.

When a defendant dies during the course of a trial and before sentencing, his-her case cannot be completed. It's common, therefore, in such cases for the government to file something called a "Nolle Prosequi," which means, loosely translated, that the government "declines to prosecute." In effect, it dismisses the case.

That's what happened with Alex after his suicide.

ACKNOWLEDGMENTS

I once read that the crux of a good story is when you throw an ordinary person into an extraordinary event. Well, if that is true, this was certainly an extraordinary event (a $350,000,000 fraud) and I was certainly an ordinary schmo. It was my dream job. After all who wouldn't want to live and work in the midst of a vineyard?

But when it all turned out to be a federal crime, I went on one of the wildest roller-coaster rides of my life. Being involved in this investigation in the way I did plays tricks on you. I went through waves of fear, fun, paranoia, exuberance, and heart pounding adrenaline—all within the same ten-minute period. Then I'd be fine and move on, or toss and turn for a night or two

But I could not have done this alone. I owe a lot to so many.

First, let me thank Bruce Bortz, publisher of Bancroft Press and his amazing assistant Jasmine Sonpar. Bruce took a chance on a first-time author and Jasmine took essentially a series of blog posts and, along with Bruce, turned them into a much better story.

I would like to thank all of you for reading this story. Writing has always been therapy for me. It allows me to organize my thoughts and beliefs in the hurricane that goes on in my head. But this was different. As I published each chapter on Substack in late 2021 and early 2022, I began to hear from so many people all over the country who were personally affected by this crime, and even from family members of some of those depicted in this book. I have met with, spoken to, and ultimately learned from so many of you. Thank you.

As Peter (again, not his real name) told me, insurance fraud is not a victimless crime. One day, thousands of people who had dutifully paid their insurance premiums each month woke up and had no insurance coverage whatsoever because their insurance provider was broke. When that happens, each individual state where the policies are sold is on the hook to pay those claims. In the Southport Lane case, thousands of policy holders in 39 states were left without insurance. That means the taxpayers in 39 states had to cover approximately $350 million in losses.

I also want to thank Michael Weinstein, the guy who always protected me, listened to me, and occasionally had to talk me down when the pressure and uncertainty were dialed up.

Special thanks to my guardians in law-enforcement: Peter (lead FBI Agent), Don (the IRS-CID agent), and Joanne (FBI).

I'm also appreciative of friends and co-workers like Jeff Leach, Brad Hoecker, Joe Coffey, Paul Doherty, Geoff Millsom, Ami Opisso, Russell Hearn, Morgant Fielder, Bo Dietl, Mike Ciravolo, my neighbor "Donnie," and Clay and Jason in Charleston, SC who checked in on me early and often.

A very special thanks to my brother Tom, who would put down the phone during a busy day and just let me talk.

All these folks—and many more—put up with me as I careened from one exceedingly high- stress moment to another, all while I trying to look like everything was fine.

Most importantly, I would like to thank my wife, Christina, and our two sons, Alex and Reid, who put up with a lot of my mood swings for several years. Sorry about that. Hopefully, writing this puts all that behind us.

But thank you most for your patience and understanding with me. As you know, I am not someone who can sit idly by and watch. I am either all in… or all out. With you guys, I am all in.

Finally, thank you to my mother, the inimitable Joan Arnold Bailey, for bugging me to write this book. Pirate Cove is for you, Mom.

ABOUT THE AUTHOR

For more than 30 years, Richard D. Bailey has been successfully providing actionable and realistic financial, management, and corporate development services to distressed public and private manufacturing, service, and distribution companies.

In 2013, Bailey was hired by Southport Lane Management (Southport), a New York-based private equity firm. Shortly after he was hired, he noticed unusual cash transfers by and between multiple Southport-owned and controlled LLCs.

Upon further investigation, Mr. Bailey uncovered critical evidence of what would turn out to be a $350 million fraud. He then worked closely with FBI investigators for several years. This resulted in four indictments and four guilty pleas. Three of the perpetrators served prison time.

In late October 2021, Alexander Chatfield Burns, the leader of the fraud, committed suicide prior to being sentenced. As a result, with millions unaccounted for, he died an innocent man.

Bailey, who's a Certified Fraud Examiner, lives in suburban Boston, Massachusetts with his wife Christina.

Bailey's *Pirate Cove* is his first book.